MOVING UP OR MOVING ON

MOVING UP OR MOVING ON

Who Advances in the Low-Wage Labor Market?

Fredrik Andersson,
Harry J. Holzer, and
Julia I. Lane

Russell Sage Foundation
New York

The Russell Sage Foundation

The Russell Sage Foundation, one of the oldest of America's general purpose foundations, was established in 1907 by Mrs. Margaret Olivia Sage for "the improvement of social and living conditions in the United States." The Foundation seeks to fulfill this mandate by fostering the development and dissemination of knowledge about the country's political, social, and economic problems. While the Foundation endeavors to assure the accuracy and objectivity of each book it publishes, the conclusions and interpretations in Russell Sage Foundation publications are those of the authors and not of the Foundation, its Trustees, or its staff. Publication by Russell Sage, therefore, does not imply Foundation endorsement.

Library of Congress Cataloging-in-Publication Data

Andersson, Fredrik, 1968–
    Moving up or moving on : who advances in the low-wage labor market? / by Fredrik Andersson, Harry J. Holzer, and Julia I. Lane.
        p.   cm.
    Includes bibliographical references and index.
    ISBN 0-87154-057-6
    1. Minimum wage—United States.   2. Working poor—United States.   3. Wages—Effect of labor mobility on—United States.   4. Labor mobility—United States.
    I. Holzer, Harry J., 1957–   II. Lane, Julia.   III. Title.
    HD4918.A59   2005
    331.12'7'0973—dc22

                                                                            2004051081

Text design by Genna Patacsil.

RUSSELL SAGE FOUNDATION
112 East 64th Street, New York, New York 10021
10   9   8   7   6   5   4   3   2   1

To our teachers and mentors
Anders Forslund, Richard Freeman, David Stevens,
who taught us to value important questions,
rigorous analysis, and good sense

Contents

About the Authors |

FREDRIK ANDERSSON is research fellow at the U.S. Census Bureau and research associate at the Urban Institute.

HARRY J. HOLZER is professor of public policy at Georgetown University, visiting fellow at the Urban Institute, and former chief economist at the U.S. Department of Labor.

JULIA I. LANE is senior research fellow at the U.S. Census Bureau, program director at the National Science Foundation, and former director of the Employment Dynamics Program at the Urban Institute.

SIMON BURGESS is professor of economics at the University of Bristol and director of the Centre for Market and Public Organisation.

ERIKA MCENTARFER is economist at the U.S. Census Bureau.

Acknowledgments |

WE HAVE RECEIVED important financial support during this project from the Employment and Training Administration (ETA) of the U.S. Department of Labor, the assistant secretary for policy and evaluation at the U.S. Department of Health and Human Services, the Rockefeller Foundation, and the Russell Sage Foundation. We would like to thank John Abowd, John Haltiwanger, and other members of the LEHD research and support staff for many years of hard work in helping to generate the data we have used here and for helpful comments on our work. Particular thanks go to Erika McEntarfer and Nick Carroll. We also thank the teams from the states participating in the LEHD program for their cooperation in providing data and for their helpful comments on earlier drafts of our research. Particular thanks go to George Putnam, Henry Jackson, Richard Holden, Phil Hardiman, and Sonya Williams. We have benefited from thoughtful comments along the way by Simon Burgess, Kelleen Kaye, Charles Michalopoulos, Mark Menchik, and Steve Wandner, as well as from helpful comments from seminar participants at the ETA research conferences in 2001 and 2003, the American Economic Association annual meetings, and the Association of Public Policy Analysis and Management annual meetings. Also helpful has been input from the staffs of the Economic Policy Institute, the U.S. Department of Health and Human Services, the Georgetown Public Policy Institute, the University of Maryland Economics Department, the University of Kentucky, the Center on Law and Social Policy, and the PEERS network.

This book reports the results of research and analysis undertaken by the U.S. Census Bureau staff. It has undergone a Census Bureau review more limited in scope than that given to official Census Bureau publications. The research is part of the Census Bureau's Longitudinal Employer-Household Dynamics (LEHD) program, which is partially supported by National Science Foundation grant SES-9978093 to the Cornell University

Institute for Social and Economic Research, the National Institute on Aging, and the Alfred P. Sloan Foundation. The views expressed here are attributable only to the authors and do not represent the views of the U.S. Census Bureau, its program sponsors, or its data providers. Some or all of the data used in this book are confidential data from the LEHD program. The Census Bureau is preparing to support external researchers' use of these data; please contact U.S. Census Bureau, LEHD Program, FB 2138-3, 4700 Silver Hill Rd., Suitland, MD 20233.

Chapter One | Introduction: Advancement and the Low-Wage Labor Market

With the passage of federal welfare reform legislation in 1996 and its subsequent implementation around the country, a lot more attention has been focused on the low-wage labor market. The focus of the old system on income maintenance has been replaced by a new emphasis on the temporary nature of cash assistance and the centrality of work.[1] Publicly funded education and training have also received less emphasis in this environment, relative to "work-first" approaches. As a result, the welfare caseload of poor single women with children has fallen dramatically, and their participation in the workforce has risen as well (see Blank 2003; Meyer and Rosenbaum 2001).[2]

But, while employment and earnings have increased for these women, new concerns have arisen about their prospects for job retention and especially advancement in the labor market. Indeed, the extent to which welfare reform has reduced poverty has been much smaller than its effects on employment thus far (see Blank 2003; for evidence on and discussion of retention and advancement issues for welfare recipients in the labor market, see Holzer and Stoll 2001; and Strawn, Greenberg, and Savner 2001). Furthermore, progress in raising employment rates among other groups—particularly low-income minority men—has been much less impressive; if anything, employment rates among less-educated men have declined rather than risen in recent years. New efforts and approaches can be found on this front as well, especially regarding specific groups such as ex-offenders in the labor market.[3]

Of course, concerns over the advancement prospects of low earners in the labor market are also not new. At least since the 1960s, much has been written by social scientists and policymakers about improving the em-

1

ployment and earnings prospects of disadvantaged workers—whether through education and training programs to increase their "human capital," or through employment programs to augment their job opportunities, or through antidiscrimination efforts to equalize the opportunities they face in the labor market (for evidence on recent trends in the labor force activity of less-educated young men, see Holzer and Offner 2002; for additional material on ex-offenders, see Travis, Soloman, and Waul 2001; and Holzer, Raphael, and Stoll 2004).

But before we consider new policies to raise employment or reduce poverty further among these groups, it would be helpful to understand more about the low-wage labor market—how it operates, whom it rewards, and what "works" for workers there in generating better employment and earnings outcomes. Despite decades of empirical research, we know surprisingly little about the low-wage labor market along certain dimensions.

To take one example, our knowledge about how workers fare in the low-wage labor market over the long term is fairly weak. Of course, some people are in this market temporarily as new labor market entrants or as workers recently displaced from better jobs (for evidence on the earnings losses experienced by displaced workers, see Jacobson, Lalonde, and Sullivan 1993).[4] Others are there voluntarily, often as students or part-time homemakers. But for those who are persistent low earners owing to weak skills, lack of job-readiness, or other labor market barriers (such as discrimination or lack of child care), relatively little is known about the extent to which they ultimately progress in this market and how they do so if and when they do.

We do know that publicly funded training programs for disadvantaged workers in the United States to date have not greatly enhanced the earnings of low-wage workers, at least partly because these programs are funded at relatively low levels in the United States, and partly because some have fairly limited effectiveness (for reviews of the evidence on the cost-effectiveness of training programs for the disadvantaged, see Lalonde 1995; Friedlander, Greenberg, and Robins 1997; Heckman, Lalonde, and Smith 1999).[5] Indeed, these limited returns to general training have led some analysts and policymakers to advocate "work-first" policies, especially for those on welfare, as the best way for them to achieve earnings gains over time. But has either approach generated much success for low-wage workers in the labor market over the long run? Are there other approaches that have had greater success?

A related set of questions involves the degree of worker attachment to specific employers over time and the extent to which such attachment leads to earnings growth. For instance, we might distinguish between labor market returns to job *retention* as opposed to job *mobility.* The former involves the returns to seniority (or "job tenure") with a particular employer and implies that workers enjoy wage growth and promotions over time owing to on-the-job training and the accumulation of skills and work experience specific to that employer. The latter involves the returns to moving to better jobs, where prospects for higher wage levels and growth are better over time. The relative returns to "job-staying" or "job-leaving" might be important pieces of information for workforce development specialists who are trying to help low earners advance in the job market. Yet, except for a few studies (which we review here), we know relatively little about these relative returns for those in the low-wage labor market.

Of course, it is also unlikely that "one size fits all" in this regard. Some workers may do better gaining additional job tenure through retention, especially if they land a good job in the first place, while others might do better by moving out of a relatively low-wage or "dead-end" job. Presumably, those who have the opportunity to move will choose (or "self-select") that option, while others will not. We would be reluctant to suggest policies based on one or the other option in general, without knowing more about the relative opportunities and preferences of the workers making these choices.

On the other hand, knowing more about the general patterns of job-staying and job-leaving in the low-wage labor market and the earnings growth associated with each type of behavior informs us about the general possibilities associated with each type of strategy. Finding differences across individuals in these patterns or "pathways" to success, by race-gender or other demographic characteristics, would further inform us about what works for different kinds of workers. Any such differences might also suggest differences in the job opportunities available to workers in various demographic groups, and part of any strategy might involve equalizing opportunities across these groups.

But what determines these opportunities in the first place? Of course, the skills that workers bring to the labor market are hugely important here. A wide range of basic skills—including both cognitive and noncognitive skills (the latter being rooted in basic attitudes toward work and in job-ready behavior)—seem relevant to earnings opportunities. The ability of low earners to gain and keep employment and to progress in the labor market also seems to reflect a range of personal characteristics and "barriers," such as physical and mental health, child care needs, and transportation problems.[6]

But once we control for whatever skills individuals bring to the low-wage labor market, their opportunities may also depend importantly on the quality of the *firms* and *jobs* to which they have access. In other words, labor market outcomes may depend not only on the characteristics and behaviors of workers on the *supply* side of the labor market but also those of the firms and jobs on the *demand* side, and especially on the interaction between the two. In the jargon of economists, the extent to which workers are "sorted" across firms and the quality of the "match" between them helps determine retention and mobility behavior as well as earnings levels and their growth over time.[7]

Since the interaction between workers and firms may be quite important, understanding the nature of these interactions in the low-wage labor market may be critical to developing appropriate policies to assist workers there. Important questions then arise, such as:

- Which low-wage workers get matched to which kinds of firms in this market?

- To what extent are differences in employment outcomes across workers explained by the quality of the firms to which they are matched?

- What are the characteristics of firms and industries that generate better outcomes for initial low earners in this market? How do these firms evolve over time, and where are they located?

- Do the pathways to success, in terms of firms and industries, vary across demographic groups, especially by race-ethnicity and gender? Do these differences suggest differential access to good firms and jobs across these groups?

- When does it make sense for low earners to change jobs, and when should they stay? Do some jobs offer better opportunities for on-the-job training and wage growth for low earners than others, and is there some trade-off between initial wage levels and their growth over time across jobs?

- Are there policy options for improving this matching process for low earners?

One set of answers to the last question might focus on the efforts of *intermediary* institutions in the labor market, which have become more important and gained more attention in recent years. These institutions play a third-party role in labor markets and help match workers to firms by providing job placement services to both. Many also provide other services to one or both parties, such as training (either general or customized to fit the needs of particular employers), work supports (such as transportation and child care assistance), or the building of "career ladders." Some, like temporary employment (or "temp") agencies, are private and for-profit firms. Others, like America Works, STRIVE, the Center for Employment and Training (CET), and QUEST, are well-known examples of private nonprofit firms in this area. Some intermediaries reflect joint union-management efforts; some focus on particular sectors of the economy (for a broad discussion of labor market intermediaries, including discussions of the programs listed here, see Giloth 2003). Although a lot of descriptive information about these intermediaries has appeared, little systematic analysis of their effects on the low-wage labor market has been undertaken to date.

Thus, a great deal remains unknown about the extent to which workers progress in the low-wage labor market over the long term, the relative effectiveness of job retention and mobility, the extent to which success and the pathways to it differ across demographic groups, the role of matches to the right kinds of firms, and the role of intermediary agencies in helping workers achieve better matches.

THE GOALS OF THE BOOK

We hope to generate at least some answers to these important questions. We will do so by analyzing the experiences of workers who have low earnings that persist for at least some period of time—in this case, three years. We will explore the extent to which their earnings grow subsequent to this initial period and the extent to which some workers "escape" the low-wage market, either partially or fully.

We are interested in whether these subsequent outcomes differ across demographic groups within the low-wage labor market. We will also explore the relative returns to staying or leaving jobs and how these experiences vary with the characteristics of firms as well as workers. We will look at the extent to which good outcomes for low earners are associated with characteristics of local geography—such as where they live and where the better jobs are located—and we will explore the evolution of these firms and jobs over time as well. Our analysis will also extend to the role of one kind of intermediary—specifically, temp agencies—in helping to match low earners to better firms.

Of course, one reason for our limited knowledge on these issues has been a lack of good data on both workers and firms. In particular, the data available on firms have been quite limited and are usually based on cross-sectional surveys at particular points in time and places, with fairly modest sample sizes. Although we have learned a great deal from these data (as we discuss later), our ability to answer the broader questions posed here depends heavily on having panel data on both workers and firms in large samples and over long periods of time. Large samples are needed to compare outcomes across many different demographic groups and different states or regions of the country; having panel data over long time periods enables us to follow the progress of initial low earners over the long term.

To our knowledge, only one dataset is available that meets all these needs: the Longitudinal Employer-Household Dynamics (LEHD) file at the U.S. Census Bureau. The LEHD data begin with the universe of state-level Unemployment Insurance (UI) wage records for a sample of states over most of the 1990s and beyond the year 2000. The UI wage records are *panel data on all individual workers and their employers* in the sectors of the economy that are covered by UI in each state. These individual records are then linked, wherever possible, to micro survey data on individuals—such as the Current Population Survey (CPS) and the Survey of Income and Program Participation (SIPP). The data are also linked on the firm side to the various economic censuses that are available.

The result is an enormous file with data on workers linked to firms over periods of several years. The data combine administrative with survey data on both sides of the market, thus generating rich information on workers and firms and the matches between them. The data have been painstakingly constructed over several years by the LEHD staff at the Census Bureau, a process that is still under way. What we present here is based on a subsample of major states for which the UI data are available over a lengthy (nine-year) period and have already been linked to household data.

THE PREVIOUS LITERATURE

Before describing the outline of this book and our general findings in the rest of this chapter (and the LEHD data in more detail in a subsequent chapter), it is worthwhile to review in a bit more detail what we have already learned from the previous research literature on low earners.

Turnover, Retention, and Earnings Growth Among Unskilled Workers

Ever since Jacob Mincer's classic treatment (1974) of the returns to labor market experience, economists have worried that high rates of job turnover might hurt the earnings progressions of low-wage workers. On the other hand, labor economists have long realized that job mobility can also play a positive role in generating earnings growth.

The extensive literature on worker turnover is reviewed in Donald Parsons (1986) and Henry Farber (1999); more recent contributions include

Ann Royalty (1998), Julia I. Lane (2000), and Harry J. Holzer and Robert J. Lalonde (2000). These works clearly demonstrate that low-skilled workers experience more job turnover than others, though the rate of turnover strongly declines with age and with tenure on the job. Furthermore, low earners are more likely than others to experience involuntary turnover— layoffs or discharges rather than quits. Their turnover is also more likely to result in a period of non-employment rather than direct movement into another job. But, conditional on an individual's skills, age, and tenure, job characteristics also seem to affect worker turnover. Thus, higher wages on the job seem to exert an independent negative effect on turnover, as do other job characteristics (for the effects of wage levels on turnover, see Parsons 1986, and Holzer and Lalonde 2000; for evidence on the effects of unionization or health insurance benefits on job turnover, see Freeman and Medoff 1984; Currie and Yelowitz 2000).

What are the effects of turnover versus job retention on the future employment and earnings of low earners? Not surprisingly, the effects of turnover are generally more negative when the turnover is involuntary (Bartel and Borjas 1981) and, similarly, when it results initially in non-employment rather than another job. Lengthy periods of non-employment not only result in earnings losses but also seem to have at least some negative effects on future wages and perhaps employment by reducing the accumulation of work experience and job tenure among low earners (for earlier evidence on how periods of non-employment affect the future wages and employment of young people, see Ellwood 1982, and Meyer and Wise 1982; for more recent evidence, see Neumark 2002; for an analysis of how periods of non-employment remain lengthy for young black men despite intervening spells of employment, see Ballen and Freeman 1986). In fact, Tricia Gladden and Christopher Taber (2000) show quite clearly that the wage returns to actual time spent working are similar (in percentage terms) for less-skilled and more-skilled young workers, but that the former experience less wage growth because they spend less time working. Nevertheless, since turnover itself responds to wage levels (and perhaps the potential for wage growth on jobs as well), the observed relationship of turnover to wages might reflect the effects of the latter on the former, as well as vice versa.

Although it is clear that the non-employment associated with turnover can be quite harmful to low earners, it is much less clear that turnover per se has negative effects. For instance, David Neumark (2002) finds quite mixed effects of turnover on the wage growth of young workers. The potentially positive effects of turnover on wages arise from the fact that voluntary moves may reflect successful mobility from lower- to higher-wage jobs. Indeed, Robert Topel and Michael Ward (1992) have demonstrated quite convincingly that a large part of early wage growth for young workers reflects mobility rather than wage growth within the same job. Unfortunately, this analysis was done on data that mostly reflect the 1960s and have never been replicated for a sample of adult low-wage workers.

The issues of turnover, retention, and wage growth also came up fairly frequently when welfare reform was being debated, as well as in its aftermath. Work by Alan Hershey and Donna Pavetti (1997) suggests that job turnover among former welfare recipients is very high, while Gary Burtless (1995) shows very little earnings growth among those leaving welfare. More recently, Harry Holzer and Michael Stoll (2001) and Holzer, Stoll, and Douglas Wissoker (2001) have shown much more retention among welfare recipients who left the rolls and were hired in the late 1990s. However, most evidence still suggests that wage growth for these women has been quite modest (for a review of this evidence, see Strawn, Greenberg, and Savner 2001; see also Cancian and Meyer 2000; Johnson 2002).

Interactions and Matching Between Workers and Firms

The research literature on the interactions between workers and firms in the low-wage labor market focuses primarily on two questions: What determines the extent to which workers with particular characteristics are matched to firms with particular characteristics? And what are the effects of these matches on worker earnings?

On the first question, a large body of work now exists that documents the varying access that minorities have to different kinds of employers. Holzer (1996) and Philip Moss and Chris Tilly (2001) have systematically explored the effects of employer skill needs, geographic location, and attitudes on the hiring of black and Latino workers. These studies followed the earlier work by William Julius Wilson (1987, 1996) and John Kasarda (1989) and the ethnographic work of Joleen Kirschenman and Kathryn Neckerman (1991), which highlighted shifting technologies, geography, and preferences on the demand side of the labor market (for the effects of changes in technology and industry structure on wages and employment more broadly, see Bound and Freeman 1992; Berman, Bound, and Griliches 1994; Autor, Katz, and Krueger 1998).

More recent work in this tradition has been done by Holzer and Stoll (2001) on employer demand for welfare recipients and by Holzer, Steven Raphael, and Stoll (2004) on demand for ex-offenders. Important work on immigrants and employers has been done by Roger Waldinger (1996), among others, that focuses on employer preferences for immigrants over native-born minorities and also on the immigrant niches or networks that develop in particular industries over time (for evidence on the stronger networks and greater success of informal job search among Latinos relative to blacks, see Falcon and Melendez 2001).

A different strand of literature focuses much less on race and ethnicity and more on the recruitment and screening methods used by employers, especially the choice between formal and informal methods; these then affect not only who gets hired but the quality of the match between worker and firm (see Rees 1966; Holzer 1987a, 1987b; Bishop 1993). In short, it is clear that less-skilled workers have differential access to employers, even controlling for their skills, based on their race-ethnicity and geographic location, and on employer attitudes and behaviors in the hiring process.

Regarding the effects of employer characteristics on wages, there has been a very long debate between those who stress the importance of worker characteristics and those who stress the effect of the job in the low-wage labor market. Recent versions of this debate have included the controversies over "dual labor markets" in the 1970s and over "efficiency wages" in the 1980s (on dual labor markets, see Doeringer and Piore 1971; on efficiency wage theories, see Katz 1986; for a broader discussion that covers both topics, see Rebitzer 1993). Aside from these controversies, empirical evidence has clearly indicated that individual workers' wages are influenced by the size, industry, unionization, and other characteristics of the firms for which they work and that the differential access of workers to employers described earlier must have consequences for their employment and earnings outcomes (see Krueger and Summers 1987; Brown, Medoff, and Hamilton 1990; Freeman and Medoff 1984).

But how much does variation across firm characteristics account for variation across workers in earnings, especially at the low end of the labor market? Until recently, the lack of extensive matched data in the United States on workers and the firms that employ them has limited our ability to fully answer this question (for reviews of this literature, see Abowd and Kramarz 1999; Haltiwanger et al. 1999). But the creation of the LEHD has enabled researchers to begin to explore these questions for the United States (for some earlier papers using the LEHD data, see Haltiwanger, Lane, and Spletzer 1999; Holzer, Lane, and Vilhuber 2003). We hope that the data presented in this volume will enable us to understand the importance of access to firms and match quality in the low-wage labor market much more clearly.

Labor Market Intermediaries

As we noted earlier, the literature on the role of intermediaries in the low-wage labor market has been largely descriptive. The available work on temp agencies is summarized in David Autor and Susan Houseman

(2002b) and in Lane and others (2003). Autor and Houseman (2002b) also document the growth of temp agencies in the labor force and demonstrated that those who work for temp agencies have lower earnings and benefit levels than do comparable workers. But whether this reflects more about the unmeasured characteristics of the workers than about the temp agencies remains unclear in this work, as does the effect of the agencies on the quality of subsequent labor market matches and outcomes for these workers. Recent work by Autor and Houseman (2002a) on the results of randomly assigning low-wage workers to temp agencies versus other services in Michigan has generated more positive outcomes associated with the temp agencies, though this work remains in progress.

More broadly, very few intermediaries have been rigorously evaluated. One exception to this is the study of the CET that is summarized in Melendez (1996). Unfortunately, this work is based only on a single site in San Jose, California. More recent attempts by the U.S. Department of Labor to replicate the CET at other sites and evaluate its effectiveness by random assignment are still under way. Other attempts to improve on worker-firm matching in the low-wage labor market, through transportation and other services, have similarly generated no clear results to date.[8] Similarly, major efforts to combine training, job placement, and other services to both workers and firms have not been rigorously evaluated.[9]

Thus, a great deal remains unknown from earlier work about pathways to earnings growth, the importance of firms, and the ability of third-party institutions to improve on the matching process between workers and firms in the low-wage labor market. This volume may help to fill these gaps to some extent.

THE OUTLINE OF THE BOOK

We present evidence in this book on how low earners did during the 1990s using the LEHD data for five states: California, Florida, Illinois, Maryland, and North Carolina.[10] These states cover a wide range of geographic regions in the United States and are quite diverse in terms of worker demographics and industrial concentrations. In chapter 2, we provide a fuller description of the LEHD data, both for these states and more broadly.

Chapter 3 looks at persistently low earners in these labor markets; by our definition, such earners are prime-age workers who have earned less than $12,000 (in 1998 dollars) for at least three consecutive years.[11] This definition is based exclusively on data from the UI wage records, plus some demographic data that have been appended to them. We consider the characteristics of both the workers themselves and the firms for which they worked during this period; the latter characteristics include industry, firm size, turnover rate, and the earnings premium that the firm provided to workers of a certain skill level. The process by which low earners are matched to firms should be better understood on the basis of this work.

In chapters 4 and 5, we provide more evidence on how persistently low earners fare in subsequent years in the labor market. In chapter 4, we analyze the extent to which low earners transition out of this status in subsequent years. This analysis focuses on individual transitions across specific (or "discrete") earnings categories—which we describe as partial or complete "escapes" out of low earnings—and it considers the characteristics of workers who make successful transitions and the characteristics of the firms for which they work. The extent to which different demographic groups of low earners achieve success with different kinds of firms is also highlighted here. Some analysis of general (or "continuous") measures of earnings growth are presented as well, using both summary data and multiple regression techniques. And as an additional check on our ability to use administrative data alone when analyzing unskilled or disadvantaged workers, we analyze subsamples of these data that are matched to the CPS, which makes more available data on workers' education, wages, and family incomes. This last analysis appears in an appendix to chapter 4.

In chapter 5, differences in success rates for job-stayers versus job-changers are highlighted, thereby enabling us to better understand the relative returns to job retention (and the accumulation of tenure) versus mobility across jobs for these workers. We also consider different combinations of retention and mobility over longer periods of time—that is, we look at the notion that it might make sense for low earners to change jobs under some circumstances (for example, if they are in dead-end jobs) and then stay in a good job when they find one. In this chapter, we also analyze the effects of work for temp agencies on subsequent success, and we consider the effects of accumulation of job tenure with any employer (as advocated in "work-first" approaches) or experience with higher-wage employers on subsequent success.

Chapter 6 presents more evidence on the firms that hire and/or advance low earners in large numbers. We consider the extent to which these characteristics vary across firms in the same industry and whether they persist over time. By better understanding these firms and their characteristics, we may gain some insights into those firms where low earners seem to be relatively more successful over time.

Chapter 7 presents data on the geographic locations of low earners versus those of other workers and the locations of lower- versus higher-wage employers. Inferences about the extent to which these spatial factors affect the matching process, and therefore the earnings prospects of low earners, are considered as well.

Finally, we summarize our findings in chapter 8 and discuss their implications for policy and for further work. Both the strengths and limitations of this analysis are discussed there as well.

OUR MAJOR FINDINGS

The major findings of this analysis can be summarized as follows:

1. *There is considerable mobility into and out of low earnings categories over time.* Of all prime-age workers who are low earners for at least three years, over half transition out of the low earnings category in the subsequent six years, but most make fairly modest progress in earnings, continuing to earn less than $15,000 a year at least some of the time. The extent of success varies across demographic groups, with white males having the highest rates of transition out of low earnings. Personal skills have important effects as well.

2. *The characteristics of employers are highly correlated with earnings and with transitions out of low-earnings status.* Working in a higher-wage industry (such as manufacturing, construction, and wholesale trade), working in a larger firm, and working in a firm with low turnover are all associated with better pay for initial low earners; working for a firm that pays positive wage premia is especially important. The sectoral pathways to success differ somewhat across race-gender groups as well: for instance, black men are underrepresented relative to whites and/or Latinos in construction and manufacturing jobs, suggesting differential access to high-quality jobs across groups.

3. *Job-changers have substantially higher rates of earnings growth over time, and higher transition rates out of low earnings, than do job-stayers.* Job changes account for most complete transitions out of low earnings and even for most partial transitions. The improved characteristics of the firms at which job-changers subsequently become employed are a major reason for these workers' relatively greater improvements in earnings. Furthermore, returns to tenure are higher at firms that pay higher wage premia than at those that pay lower wages, reinforcing the benefits of moving to higher-wage employers. On the other hand, job retention can be important as well: the highest earnings gains among low earners are achieved by those who transition to better employers early and then accumulate more tenure in these newer jobs.

4. *Low earners who work for temp agencies have higher earnings in subsequent jobs.* Furthermore, this effect is totally accounted for by the quality of the jobs that these workers hold in subsequent periods. Temp agencies

thus appear to improve the quality of subsequent job matches for low earners. There are also some general returns to accumulating tenure on any earlier job (though these are relatively small) and for working earlier at a high-wage firm.

5.   *The characteristics and behaviors of particular firms affect opportunities for low earners, as do their geographic locations.* Even within detailed industries in particular states, there is a great deal of heterogeneity in terms of which firms hire low earners and provide them with opportunities to advance. But the firms that provide these opportunities do so persistently, and so they can be identified on the basis of past performance. Low earners are located farther away from good job opportunities than are nonlow earners, and these geographic differences suggest that the access of low earners to good jobs is limited by spatial factors in metropolitan areas.

Taken together, these findings suggest that, while training and skill remediation are important, the process by which workers are matched to firms in the low-wage labor market also has large and important effects on the outcomes we observe for these workers. Policies that seek to improve the access of low earners to higher-wage firms and industries could have major payoffs. Job placement and training policies for low earners need to be better integrated, and sequential employment strategies should perhaps be developed for moving low earners across jobs in ways that generate better earnings growth for them. The results on temp agencies also suggest that these firms—and perhaps intermediary institutions more broadly—could play an important and positive role in improving the earnings of these workers over time.

Chapter Two | The Longitudinal Employer-Household Dynamics (LEHD) Program Data

MOST EMPIRICAL ANALYSES of the low-wage labor market have been constrained by the types of data usually available. Clearly, analysis of worker-based surveys results in greater in-depth understanding about the relationship between worker characteristics and labor market outcomes, and analysis of employer-based surveys results in similar understandings of the employer side of the market. But neither analysis alone gives us much insight into the interactions between the two sides of the labor market. In addition, since many surveys either are only cross-sectional in nature or have a relatively short time span for follow-up, their usefulness for helping us understand the long-term employment dynamics of the poor can be quite limited.

The data used in this book, however, enable us to capture the dynamic interaction of workers and firms for just under a decade—from 1993 to 2001—and represent the first large-scale attempt to exploit the development of an entirely new database infrastructure at the U.S. Census Bureau in the analysis of low-wage work.

Because these data are very new and their structure is not generally well known, we devote part of this chapter to describing the nature of the dataset and the key data concepts used in the analysis, and we compare the coverage of the database with that of the 2000 decennial census. In addition, because we are also introducing some new measures of worker and firm quality, we provide a fairly detailed discussion of these measures as well as indications of how they have changed over time.

THE LEHD DATABASE INFRASTRUCTURE

The LEHD program was established at the Census Bureau in 1998 in response to the need to provide more information on economic dynamics without increasing respondent burden or significantly increasing taxpayer burden. The program draws on already existing survey and administrative data from both the demographic and economics directorates at the bureau and integrates them with Unemployment Insurance (UI) wage record data from twenty-two partner states, of which five are used here. This integration, which takes place under strict confidentiality protection protocols (described later in this chapter), appears diagrammatically in figure 2.1.

Briefly, state UI wage records sit at the core of these data. These records, which consist of reports filed by employers every quarter for each individual in covered employment, permit the construction of a database that provides longitudinal information on workers, firms, and the match between the two. The coverage is roughly 96 percent of private nonfarm wage and salary employment; the coverage of agricultural and federal government employment is less comprehensive. Self-employed individuals and independent contractors are also not covered. Although the administrative records themselves are subject to some error, staff at the LEHD program have invested substantial resources in cleaning the records and making them internally consistent (for a description of the approach, see Abowd and Vilhuber 2004).

Figure 2.1   The Longitudinal Employer-Household Dynamics Program

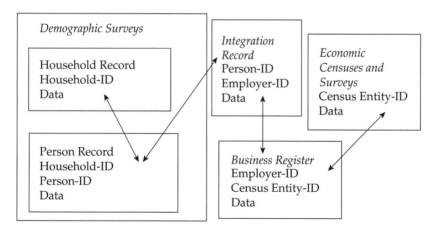

Source: Authors' compilation.

The Census Bureau information used in this study consists primarily of basic demographic information: date of birth, place of birth, sex, and a crude measure of race and ethnicity. This information is available for almost all workers in the dataset—the nonmatch rate is about 4 percent. The UI wage records have also been matched with the Current Population Survey (CPS), but since this is clearly a cross-sectional match, we simply use it as a consistency check in the research.

There are clearly many advantages associated with this integrated database—its enormous sample size, its longitudinal structure, and the information it provides on employer-employee matches. There are also some disadvantages. One is that employers typically do not report hours or weeks worked. Another is that it is impossible to discern whether multiple jobs, when held within a quarter, are held sequentially or at the same time. We address both of these issues by creating a measure of annualized earnings for each individual in the dataset *at the primary employer* in each year that they appear in the data. That is, for the entire year that an individual appears in a state, we identify his or her primary employer as the one that pays that individual the highest earnings in that year.

There are two additional conceptual issues to be addressed. One is the distinction between "firms" and "establishments": the latter are specific places of business and employment, while the former are the overall legal entities that sometimes encompass multiple places of business. Although in our work we typically refer to the employer as a "firm," the actual reporting unit in the data is an administrative rather than an economic entity; in other words, the filing unit reflects an employer identification number rather than a specific firm. The distinction is immaterial for the approximately 70 percent of workers who work for single-establishment employers. But for those who work for a multiple-establishment employer, it is really not clear whether they are working for the firm or for an establishment.

The other conceptual issue is that of earnings. According to the *Bureau of Labor Statistics Handbook of Methods* (U.S. Department of Labor 1997), UI wage records measure "gross wages and salaries, bonuses, stock options, tips, and other gratuities, and the value of meals and lodging, where supplied." They do not include employer contributions to OASDI (old age, survivor, and disability insurance), health insurance, workers' compensation, unemployment insurance, and private pension and welfare funds.

Given the sensitive nature of the dataset, it is worth discussing the confidentiality protection in some detail. All data that are brought into the LEHD system have been made anonymous, in the sense that standard identifiers and names are stripped off and replaced by a unique protected identification key (PIK). Only Census Bureau employees or individuals who have special sworn status are permitted to work with the data; not only have they undergone an FBI check, but they also are subject to a $250,000 fine and/or five years in jail if the identity of an individual or business is disclosed. All projects have to be reviewed by the Census Bureau and other data custodians, and any tables or regression results that are released are subject to full disclosure review.

THE CREATION AND INTERPRETATION OF INDIVIDUAL AND FIRM FIXED EFFECTS

Most people know intuitively that earnings are affected by two main factors: who you are and where you work, or what economists call individual characteristics and firm characteristics. It thus makes sense that some policies to improve earnings outcomes have focused on the individual side and others on the firm side. A great deal of work has been done on the effects of changing individual characteristics such as education and training on the transition of workers out of low-wage work. Other work has focused on the firm side and examined the effect of different placement strategies: placing workers in different types of firms and jobs. Yet one of the most difficult challenges that policymakers face is separating out the two effects in a statistical framework.

One of the major advantages of the LEHD data is that the two separate effects have been statistically distinguished, and we take advantage of this extensively in this book. Here we describe how we calculate and interpret these effects—what economists call the person and firm "fixed effects."

A full description of how they are calculated is provided in John Abowd, Paul Lengermann, and Kevin McKinney (2003). Since we have panel data on both workers and firms, these effects are drawn from a regression of an annualized measure of earnings on dummy variables for each worker and each firm in a sample that includes all person-quarters of UI-covered employment in each of our states during the 1990s.[1] The coefficients on these respective dummy variables are then appended to the data and used as independent variables in our analysis on a subset of these data.

How can these coefficients be interpreted? The person fixed effects can be thought of as the market value of the portable component of an individual's skills and attitudes. These fixed effects have two components: an individual or person effect, which does not vary over time, and a component based on labor market experience. The individual effect includes some factors that are often observable to the statistician, such as years of education and sex, and some factors that are often not observable, such as innate ability, "people skills," problem-solving skills, perseverance, family background, and educational quality.

The intuitive explanation for this quantitative measure is that it captures the average market value that employers assign an individual as that individual moves from firm to firm. Note that this measure is not an arbitrary skill measure, such as years of education or occupation, that may or may not be the correct measure of how the market values skills. If, for example, an individual is a highly skilled blacksmith and the market does not value this skill, the person effect is correspondingly low. If the individual is physically extremely strong and the value of this quality is decreasing in the marketplace, the individual also has a relatively low person effect. But if, for example, the individual scores highly on problem-solving skills and this is valued in the marketplace, then she or he has a high person effect. As such, these are likely to be "better" measures of skills in a more complex economy. Indeed, the case study evidence (see, for example, Appelbaum, Bernhardt, and Murnane 2003) suggests that years of education is simply not an adequate measure of human capital in a service economy.

The firm fixed effect similarly captures a variety of factors. Most simplistically, it captures the premium or discount that a given firm pays workers on average, controlling for their individual characteristics. This premium might be due to a higher level of capital in the firm, which would clearly increase the productivity of individual workers. Or it might be due to unionization—the transportation equipment industry, for example, has a relatively high average firm fixed effect. It might also be a compensating differential—the average firm fixed effect in the mining industry presumably is high in order to compensate workers for the riskiness and unpleasantness of mine work. Finally, the firm effect captures a range of human resource policies chosen by the firm, including the effects of training and promotion policies as well as compensation.

Two points are important to make here. First, the person fixed effect is not the same as a person's wage. In our analysis of wages, we decompose fixed effects into three parts: a person effect, a firm effect, and an unexplained residual. Because the person effect and the firm effect are virtually uncorrelated, when measured at the level of an individual job individuals' earnings may be due to who they are or where they work.

This is illustrated in table 2.1, which presents the total wage differences (relative to the mean) for a group of very high-paying and low-paying industries and then decomposes these differences into person and firm effects. Clearly the highest-paying industry—security, commodity, and brokers, and services—is high-paying both because it has high-quality workers and because firms within that industry firms pay a premium to those workers. However, another highly paid industry—electricity, gas, and sanitary services—has high wages entirely because firms in the industry pay their workers much higher than average. The workers themselves are of the same quality as the rest of the workforce. Similar results are evi-

Table 2.1   Sources of Industry Earnings Differentials

Standard Industrial Classification	Industry	Industry Wage Premium	Premium Attributable to Person Effects	Premium Attributable to Firm Effects
Highest-paying industries				
62	Security, commodity, brokers, and services	82%	34%	37%
67	Holding and other investments	70	34	27
48	Communication	63	7	52
49	Electric, gas, and sanitary services	54	0	55
81	Legal services	54	18	31
Lowest-paying industries				
58	Eating and drinking places	−45	−12	−38
01	Agriculture-crops	−35	−10	−31
72	Personal services	−33	−12	−24
79	Amusement and recreation services	−32	−8	−28
70	Hotel and lodging services	−32	−17	−19
54	Food stores	−30	1	−30

Source: LEHD data for California, Florida, Illinois, and North Carolina, 1992 to 1999. Table adapted from Abowd (2002).

denced when low-wage industries are analyzed in the second set of panels. Eating and drinking establishments, for example, hire workers of lower than average quality and pay them less. However, in another very low-wage industry, food stores, firms actually hire workers of above-average quality but just pay them less.

The second point is that these new measures are important. Traditional surveys of workers that measure the "kitchen sink" of demographic characteristics—such as education, occupation, age, sex, marital status, and even some firm characteristics such as firm size and industry—are typically able to explain some 30 percent of earnings variation. With longitudinal data on workers and firms, we can explain nearly 90 percent of earnings variation in some specifications (Abowd 2002).

Of course, the estimation of these person and firm fixed effects must rely on certain assumptions that are frequently made in the empirical literature using panel data.[2] Furthermore, while these data have enormous advantages relative to those used more frequently in labor market analysis, they also have a number of limitations. As noted earlier, we cannot distinguish between hourly wages and hours or weeks worked per quarter; thus, we cannot distinguish with any certainty those people choosing to work part-time from those working full-time at low compensation. Without data on various individual and family characteristics (such as education and family income or numbers of earners in the household), it is also difficult to focus on those who are disadvantaged. We deal with these problems later, partly through the design of our sample and partly by replicating our results on limited subsamples of our data that are linked to the Current Population Survey and for which the key individual and family characteristics are available.

COMPARING THE LEHD DATA TO OTHER SOURCES

Because the LEHD data are quite new, and because we analyze only a subset of states, it is worth spending some time comparing the characteristics of workers in the LEHD dataset with the characteristics of a more familiar dataset, the 2000 decennial census. We report the results of the comparison in table 2.2.

Briefly, the demographic characteristics of the workforce in the LEHD data are very similar to those of the decennial census, with some important differences. The LEHD data have a higher proportion of younger workers overall (about 20 percent) than do either the five-state census sample or the full census; this difference may be due to coverage and reporting differences. The five states we are studying have a lower proportion of white workers than does the country at large—about 66 percent here rather than 78 percent for the nation. The industry distribution is, by and large, very similar, although the LEHD data show more workers in professional services and fewer in educational, health, and social services. The earnings in the five states are typically slightly higher than for the country at large, but the LEHD earnings measures are slightly lower, probably owing primarily to the coverage differences mentioned earlier.

One of the most important advantages of the LEHD dataset is the sheer size of the sample, which is well illustrated in table 2.3. The total sample in our overall dataset—which is subset to include only workers twenty-five to fifty-four years old who earn more than $2,000 per year—averages about 37 million individuals per year and almost 2 million firms, for a total of 142

Table 2.2 Distribution of Workers Across Demographics and Industries: LEHD Data and Census 2000 Data

| | Census 2000 | | | | | | LEHD Data | |
| | Nationwide | | Five States | | | | | |
	Distribution	Earnings	Distribution	Earnings			Distribution	Earnings
All	1.00	$31,780	1.00	$33,026			1.00	$29,598
By gender								
Male	0.53	38,459	0.54	39,510			0.52	36,208
Female	0.47	24,110	0.46	25,477			0.48	22,455
By age group								
24 and younger	0.14	11,571	0.14	11,809			0.20	8,929
25 to 54	0.72	35,528	0.72	36,796			0.67	34,832
55 and older	0.15	33,518	0.15	34,957			0.13	33,560
By race-ethnicity								
White	0.78	33,930	0.67	36,863			0.66	34,190
Black	0.09	25,776	0.10	26,347			0.14	19,255
Asian	0.03	34,458	0.06	34,938			0.06	30,355
Hispanic	0.10	21,756	0.17	22,415			0.14	17,956
By NAICS sector								
Agriculture, forestry, fishing, and so on	0.02	14,985	0.02	16,589			0.02	11,506
Mining	0.00	44,600	0.00	43,965			0.00	48,158
Transportation and warehousing	0.05	36,606	0.05	36,893			0.04	33,682

(Table continues on p. 22.)

Table 2.2 (Continued)

| | Census 2000 | | | | LEHD Data | |
| | Nationwide | | Five States | | | |
	Distribution	Earnings	Distribution	Earnings	Distribution	Earnings
Construction	0.07	29,315	0.07	30,613	0.06	28,363
Manufacturing	0.15	38,442	0.13	39,740	0.12	41,660
Wholesale trade	0.04	37,892	0.04	38,510	0.05	40,283
Retail trade	0.12	23,606	0.12	25,120	0.13	19,259
Information	0.03	42,476	0.03	45,763	0.03	51,914
Finance, insurance, and real estate; rental, and leasing	0.07	42,810	0.07	43,520	0.06	43,497
Professional services	0.09	37,623	0.10	38,580	0.15	29,295
Educational, health, and social services	0.20	30,079	0.19	31,340	0.16	29,198
Entertainment, food, and accommodation	0.08	16,950	0.08	18,231	0.10	12,774
Other services	0.05	20,435	0.05	20,403	0.04	18,144
Public administration	0.05	38,410	0.05	41,320	0.03	36,155

Source: Authors' compilation.

Table 2.3   Characteristics of the Dataset

Year	Number of Workers	Number of Firms	Quarterly Observations	Workers 25 to 54 Years Old Earning More Than $2,000	Workers 25 to 54 Years Old Earning More Than $2,000 in Year t − 1, t, and t + 1	Primary Firms of Workers in Column 5
1993	33,610,480	1,611,313	125,958,556	20,841,562	—	—
1994	34,446,998	1,637,966	131,241,944	21,166,665	17,127,531	1,160,274
1995	35,235,729	1,667,450	134,616,936	21,414,898	—	—
1996	35,904,821	1,701,738	138,824,383	21,596,830	—	—
1997	36,784,149	1,765,017	141,280,177	21,885,636	17,711,051	1,235,889
1998	37,737,586	1,784,740	146,436,574	22,122,646	—	—
1999	38,700,090	1,830,721	150,383,219	22,289,055	—	—
2000	39,824,157	1,872,866	154,238,335	22,476,714	17,997,147	1,235,889
2001	40,475,026	1,909,504	156,754,546	22,657,380	—	—
Average	36,968,782	1,753,479	142,192,741	21,827,932	17,611,910	1,210,684
Sum	332,719,036	15,781,315	1,279,734,670	196,451,386	52,835,729	3,632,052

Source: LEHD data for California, Florida, Illinois, and North Carolina.

million observations (which reflect employer-employee matches, or person-job combinations). When we subset the dataset, however, to examine only workers with a three-year attachment criterion (see chapter 3) and focus on the primary employer-employee match rather than on all matches, the dataset averages about 18 million individuals and just over 1 million firms per period, for a total sample size of about 36 million records.

CONCLUSIONS

In this chapter, we provided an overview of the structure of the LEHD data and the new measures—individual and firm fixed effects—that have been constructed by LEHD staff. The longitudinal nature of the data, combined with the fact that they represent the universe of workers and firms in each state, permits a rich new analysis of both the interactions between workers and firms and the effects of job transitions. The demographic characteristics of the workforce, as well as the industrial characteristics of the employers, are very similar to those in the most comprehensive alternative data source, the 2000 decennial census.

Chapter Three | Who Are the Low Earners and What Are Their Jobs?

As WE NOTED earlier, our goal in this volume is to follow a set of low earners over time in the labor market and look at how their earnings evolve as they interact with various employers. The LEHD data that we described in the previous chapter are uniquely well suited to this purpose. They enable us to look at both low earners and the firms for which they work; moreover, the samples are large enough that we can look at many demographic subgroups, and with many years of data we can also analyze dynamics over time.

Before we proceed with this analysis, we need to define exactly what we mean by low earners in this context. We cannot define low earners on the basis of educational attainment or family income, since these characteristics are not available for most individuals in the LEHD data. Instead, we use a definition based on annual earnings of individual workers over a period of three years. Once we define low earners, we look carefully at their demographic characteristics, such as age, race-ethnicity, gender, and whether they were born in the United States or elsewhere. Though years of education is not available for most workers (except for the small subsamples matched to the CPS and other household surveys), we have computed a personal "fixed effect" for each individual—which, as we noted in chapter 2, we interpret as a measure of his or her long-term skills and earnings capacity.

We also analyze the characteristics of the firms for which these low earners work. We consider the easily observed characteristics of firms, such as their industry, size, and turnover rates, and then look at the firm "fixed effect," defined as the wage premium paid by firms regardless of the characteristics of the workers whom they employ. We show that the firms at which people work vary by their race-ethnicity, gender, and place of birth as well as by their earnings capacity. The process by which workers are "matched" to their employers is, in our view, a major determinant of their employment opportunities over time, and one that we want to understand in some detail.

Having thus defined low earners and the firms for which they work, we move on in subsequent chapters to consider the evolution of their earnings over time and the role played in this process by the various employers for whom they work.

DEFINING LOW EARNERS

A variety of difficulties arise when we attempt to define low earners on the basis of administrative data on quarterly and annual earnings only. For one thing, we cannot separate those with low wages from those with a low number of hours worked per week or a low number of weeks worked per quarter. Thus, it is difficult to separate those who are *voluntarily* choosing to work part-time—such as students, homemakers, and the elderly—from those who work full-time but at low wages. Furthermore, we want to separate those with *transitory* earnings difficulties—such as those returning to the labor market after a lengthy absence or those who have recently been displaced from a job—from those with *persistent* earnings difficulties over some number of years. On the other hand, we also want to define these difficulties in a way that allows for improvements over a longer period of time.

To deal with these potential problems, we limit ourselves to a sample of prime-age workers—those age twenty-five to fifty-four—at the beginning of our period of analysis (1993). In doing so, we largely eliminate certain groups, such as students and the elderly (and near-elderly), who often voluntarily choose to work part-time. Though some groups of voluntary part-time workers, such as homemakers, no doubt remain in our sample, we analyze most results separately by gender and race-ethnicity, thereby separating groups with many voluntary part-time workers (such as white females) from others that presumably have fewer. Also, to ensure that those whom we observe in our sample are at least marginally attached to the labor market, we require that individuals worked for at least one quarter in each year, earning at least $2,000 that year.[1] This last requirement may eliminate from our sample some workers who encountered severe barriers to work, but it seems reasonable in light of our focus on labor market advancement rather than employment per se.

Within our sample of prime-age workers, we define persistent low earners as *those who earned $12,000 per year or less for each of three years during the period 1993 to 1995.*[2] The three-year period that we use to define low earnings is long enough that we generally avoid those with strictly transitory problems and can focus instead on those with persistent low earnings. On the other hand, choosing a three-year period as a base period in which to define low earnings leaves us with six years subsequent to this period—or two subsequent three-year periods, 1996 to 1998 and 1999 to 2001—during which we can observe earnings growth and dynamics over time for our sample of initial low earners.

The $12,000 cutoff for low earnings may seem somewhat arbitrary. However, we have deliberately chosen a level of earnings that defines poverty-level income for a family of four in which there are no other earners. Even allowing for receipt of the Earned Income Tax Credit (EITC), $12,000 in annual earnings leaves such a family below the poverty line in income.[3] Furthermore, we have analyzed the education levels and family incomes for a small subset of workers who were matched to the Current Population Survey in at least one of the years available. Using different earnings cutoffs, we could identify the levels of earnings at which most workers have limited educational attainment and fairly modest family incomes. The results of this exercise indicated that, even at $12,000 in earnings, most low earners did not have family incomes below the poverty line, and at least some had postsecondary education. But most low earners by this definition had family incomes below 200 percent of the poverty line, and most had only high school diplomas or less.[4] Thus, the $12,000 cutoff generates a sample of workers whose personal and family characteristics approximate those in which we are most interested.

Of course, small or transitory increases in earnings above this cutoff do not necessarily imply labor market success. So we also define two intermediate categories of earnings: *partially low earnings*—earnings above $12,000 in one or more years in the period 1993 to 1995 but never more than $15,000; and *partially nonlow earnings*—earnings above $15,000 but not consistently over the three-year period. Those with consistently nonlow earnings are thus those with earnings above $15,000 in each of the three years during this period. Although this is not a particularly high level of earnings, it would have enabled a family of four to have enough income—along with the Earned Income Tax Credit but no other earnings— to rise above the federal poverty line.

We thus have a definition of low earnings with four categories during our base period. When we compare the earnings of these workers in subsequent three-year periods, we can define *transition rates* (or probabilities) across these categories, conditional on whichever earnings category the individual was in during the three-year base period. Those who were initially low earners are considered "partial escapers" out of the low-wage labor market if in subsequent periods they had partially low or partially nonlow earnings, and they are considered "complete escapers" if they consistently earned above $15,000 in subsequent years.

Of course, the same individual might have held several jobs with several different firms during any three-year period, thereby complicating our efforts to analyze the characteristics of the firms for which low earners worked. To simplify this part of the analysis we define each individual's *primary* employer over each three-year period as the one with which they had the highest earnings per quarter for the largest number of quarters during the time period. When comparing across three-year periods, we can also distinguish primary *job-changers* from *job-stayers:* the former group includes those whose primary employers differed across three-year periods, and the latter group includes those whose primary employers were the same.

Finally, we note that any such analysis across earnings categories is limited by the fact that the categories, at best, are somewhat arbitrarily drawn. Thus, we supplement our analysis of low earners and their movements across earnings categories whenever possible by also considering more general (or more continuous) measures of earnings—both annual and quarterly—as well as measures of quarters employed and number of jobs held. In subsequent chapters, we analyze changes in these broader earnings and employment measures, as well as movements across our earnings categories. The portrait of low earners and their employers that emerges therefore does not depend on any particular categorizing scheme with respect to low earnings.

The analysis in the remainder of this chapter focuses on the numbers and characteristics of low earners as well as the characteristics of their employers during the base period for our analysis, the years 1993 to 1995.

LOW EARNERS AND THEIR CHARACTERISTICS

We begin by exploring the numbers and personal characteristics of low earners during the base period in our sample of states. Figure 3.1 presents the distribution of prime-age workers in our sample across the four earnings categories defined earlier. The figure indicates that about two-thirds of working adults were nonlow earners: they consistently earned above $15,000 a year. But one-third of these adults had low earnings (under $12,000 per year) at least some of the time, and nearly 8 percent were persistently low earners by this definition. This is the group we focus on most closely in our analysis.

To get a better sense of what these categories mean in terms of earnings levels and employment rates, we present additional data in table 3.1. For

Figure 3.1   Distribution of Prime-Age Workers Across Earnings
Categories, 1993 to 1995

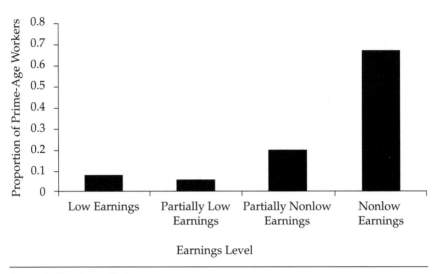

Source: Authors' compilation.
Note: The earnings categories are defined in the text.

all prime-age workers in the relevant period, and then separately for each
of our four earnings categories, we present means and medians for six
measures of employment outcomes: annual earnings, quarterly earnings,
full quarterly earnings (defined as earnings for those individuals who
were employed for the entire quarter with the same employer), number of
quarters worked over the three-year period, number of full quarters
worked, and number of employers.

The data there give us a better sense of the labor market experiences
and outcomes of persistently low earners, and how they compare with
other workers. We find that, on average, low earners had annual earnings
of about $7,000 per year and $2,000 per quarter worked (about $2,200 for
full quarters). Each of these measures is substantially below what we find
for workers in other categories, including the partially low and partially
nonlow earners.[5] The full distribution of earnings for low earners also suggests that very few hovered just below the $12,000 cutoff, so that our por-
trait of them is not highly sensitive to small changes in the categories that
we have defined.[6]

As for employment levels, the data indicate that our low earners generally worked ten to eleven quarters during the three-year period. This level

Table 3.1 Earnings and Employment, by Earnings Categories

	Low Earnings		Partially Low Earnings		Partially Nonlow Earnings		Nonlow Earnings	
	Mean	Median	Mean	Median	Mean	Median	Mean	Median
Total annual earnings	$7,081	$7,099	$11,011	$11,188	$17,916	$16,053	$45,430	$35,878
Quarterly earnings	2,076	2,083	3,029	3,027	5,257	4,468	11,730	9,187
Full quarterly earnings	2,226	2,212	3,187	3,157	5,663	4,761	11,558	9,175
Quarters of employment	10.42	11.00	10.97	12.00	10.54	11.00	11.75	12.00
Full quarters of employment	7.61	8.00	8.58	9.00	7.91	8.00	10.84	12.00
Number of employers	2.85	2.00	2.58	2.00	2.61	2.00	1.54	1.00

Source: Authors' compilation.

Note: The earnings categories are defined in the text. Earnings are presented in 1998 dollars using CPI-U as the deflator. "Full quarters" are defined as all quarters in which an individual's employer is the same as in both the preceding and following quarters.

of employment is hardly different from what we observe for other earnings categories, though it is also partly a result of our sample definition, which requires at least marginal attachment of each worker in each year. Of course, quarterly employment is a very crude measure of employment levels, since it can represent as little as one day of work or as much as thirteen full weeks. In this regard, our measure of "full quarters worked" (that is, the number of quarters in which an individual worked for the same employer as in the earlier and later quarters) is a somewhat better indicator of consistent employment outcomes. Perhaps not surprisingly, this measure shows that low earners had fewer full quarters of employment—about eight on average—than did other categories of earners. We also find that, in general, they had had two to three employers over the three-year period, which is considerably more than what we find for nonlow earners. Thus, their employment histories suggest somewhat greater instability and less time spent working than what we observe for other groups, as well as considerably lower earnings when they did work for the full quarter.

How do different demographic groups of workers differ in their tendency to be low earners and in their employment outcomes more broadly? These questions are answered in table 3.2. We present the percentage of each group that falls into the category of low earners, as well as our general measures of earnings and employment outcomes, for each of several demographic subgroups. The subgroups are defined by gender, race-ethnicity, place of birth (U.S.- versus foreign-born), and age group.

Our results indicate, not surprisingly, that some demographic groups were much more likely to be persistent low earners than others. For instance, females within each racial-ethnic group were more likely to be low earners than males. Thus, a *gender gap* in earnings is easily detectable among all race-ethnic groups. But among whites the gender gap is much more pronounced than it is among other groups: 10 percent of white females but only 3 percent of white males had low earnings. Similarly, the racial gaps in earnings among men are wider than among women. Among other factors, this probably indicates that white females were more likely than minority females to choose part-time employment when they were in the labor force (see, for example, Blank 1998).

Comparing across the minority groups, we find that Hispanic females were considerably more likely to be low earners than any other group; this is less true for Hispanic men. Asian men and women, on average, had higher earnings than their black and Hispanic counterparts, but lower earnings than whites (at least among men). Also, foreign-born workers generally had lower earnings than did those born in the United States, but similar employment stability (measured again by full quarters of employment and number of employers over three years).

Table 3.2   Earnings and Employment, by Demographic Group

	Fraction in Each Group Who Are Low Earners	Mean of Total Annual Earnings	Quarters of Employment	Full Quarters of Employment	Number of Employers
All workers	0.08	$34,781	11.37	9.89	1.91
By race-ethnicity and gender					
White females	0.10	28,732	11.43	10.07	1.80
Black females	0.12	23,948	11.42	9.87	2.11
Asian females	0.08	28,762	11.39	10.07	1.88
Hispanic females	0.16	20,414	11.30	9.79	1.92
White males	0.03	46,465	11.35	9.90	1.85
Black males	0.09	27,868	11.26	9.37	2.43
Asian males	0.07	34,524	11.26	9.70	1.99
Hispanic males	0.09	23,101	11.21	9.37	2.30
By age					
25 to 34	0.08	27,640	11.28	9.47	2.22
35 to 44	0.07	37,036	11.40	10.03	1.81
45 to 54	0.07	41,970	11.44	10.31	1.60
By place of birth					
Foreign-born	0.10	29,144	11.28	9.75	1.98
U.S.-born	0.07	35,912	11.38	9.92	1.90

Source: Authors' compilation.

The gaps across groups in average earnings and employment generally mirror those found in the frequencies of low earners. But we find that blacks and Hispanics seemed to lag behind their counterparts in quarters of full employment and that blacks generally had had larger numbers of employers than had other groups. The data thus imply *a greater instability and lower frequency of employment among blacks, and especially black men,* compared to other groups, while employment experience among Hispanics and especially Asians appears more stable. Of course, these findings reflect differences in employment rates across ethnic groups that have often been noted elsewhere (see, for example, Holzer and Offner 2002). Not surprisingly, we also find that average earnings and employment outcomes vary with age: even among prime-age workers, younger adults (those age twenty-five to thirty-four) had lower earnings and employment than did those age thirty-five to fifty-four.

To what extent do these differences in employment outcomes across groups reflect the differences in the earnings capacities of workers in these

Figure 3.2   Fractions of Workers in Each Person Effect Quartile Who
Are Low Earners

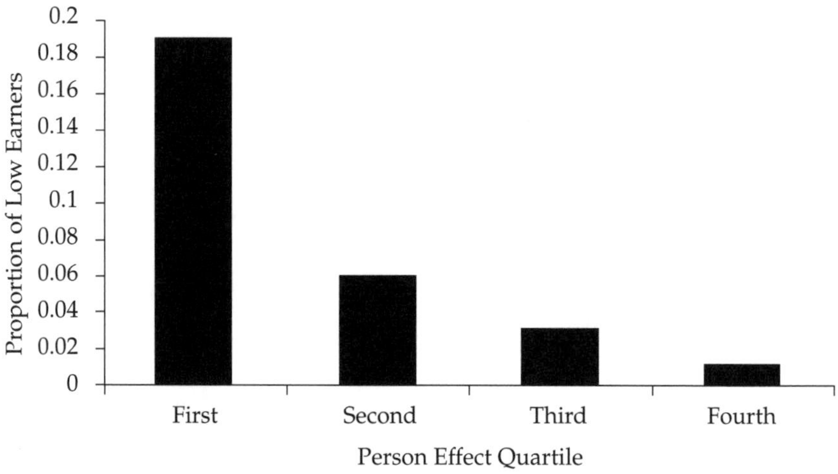

Source: Authors' compilation.

groups that stem from differences in skills and other relatively permanent characteristics? To answer this question we focus on the person fixed effects we have calculated for each worker. As we noted in chapter 2, the estimated fixed effect for each person should capture any permanent characteristics (such as basic skills, physical and mental health, attitudes, and so on) that are determinants of their earnings capacity over time.

In figure 3.2, we plot the tendency of workers to be low earners according to their quartile of the fixed-effects distribution. We find that much greater fractions of those in the lowest fixed-effects quartile were lower earners than was true in any other quartile; in fact, the figures imply that a strong majority of low earners (over 60 percent) were concentrated among those with low person fixed effects. Of course, this is at least partly due to the fact that the period over which we have estimated these effects generally includes the base years on which we now focus when calculating earnings status—in other words, the fixed effect is somewhat endogenous to our definition of low earnings. On the other hand, this overlap does not completely account for this strong correlation and suggests a strong degree of permanence in the low earnings of many such workers.[7]

Table 3.3 presents some additional evidence on the characteristics and employment outcomes of workers according to their person fixed effects.

Table 3.3   Demographics of Workers and Earnings Across Quartiles of Person Fixed Effects

| | Quartile of Person Fixed Effect | | | | |
	First	Second	Third	Fourth	All
Distribution of Workers by Demographic Groups					
All workers	0.25	0.25	0.25	0.25	1.00
By race-ethnicity and gender					
White females	0.26	0.24	0.25	0.25	1.00
Black females	0.31	0.30	0.25	0.15	1.00
Asian females	0.26	0.25	0.25	0.25	1.00
Hispanic females	0.33	0.26	0.23	0.17	1.00
White males	0.19	0.24	0.26	0.30	1.00
Black males	0.38	0.29	0.21	0.12	1.00
Asian males	0.27	0.23	0.24	0.26	1.00
Hispanic males	0.31	0.29	0.25	0.16	1.00
By age					
25 to 34	0.07	0.19	0.33	0.41	1.00
35 to 44	0.26	0.31	0.24	0.19	1.00
45 to 54	0.50	0.25	0.14	0.10	1.00
By place of birth					
Foreign-born	0.33	0.26	0.22	0.19	1.00
U.S.-born	0.23	0.25	0.26	0.26	1.00
Mean Employment and Earnings					
Total annual earnings	$19,693	$28,450	$34,724	$58,112	$35,245
Quarterly earnings	5,179	7,415	9,028	15,395	9,254
Full quarterly earnings	5,278	7,530	9,126	15,129	9,265
Quarters of employment	11.29	11.38	11.42	11.39	11.37
Full quarters of employment	9.67	9.88	9.99	10.09	9.91
Number of different employers	2.01	1.94	1.88	1.71	1.88

Source: Authors' compilation.

The first panel presents the distribution of demographic subgroups across the fixed effects quartiles, while the second panel presents the average earnings and employment outcomes associated with each quartile of person fixed effects.

The results in the first panel indicate that person fixed effects do vary systematically across race-ethnic and gender groups. Not surprisingly, white males were the group least likely to have low person fixed effects, while blacks and Hispanics were the most likely to fall into that category. Indeed, black males were more heavily concentrated among those with low person fixed effects than any other group. Those who were foreign-born were also considerably more likely to have low person fixed effects than those born in the United States. Unfortunately, the extent to which these differences across racial groups reflect differences in skills rather than discrimination or other sources of relatively permanent disadvantage for minorities cannot be determined here. Likewise, gender gaps could reflect discrimination or the relatively greater preferences of males for full-time employment.

Not surprisingly, the second panel indicates that average annual and quarterly earnings in our three-year base period are highly correlated with the person fixed-effects category. Somewhat more interestingly, the number of quarters employed—both overall and fully—and the number of employers show somewhat less variation across these categories, indicating that those with low fixed effects do not necessarily work less consistently than those with more positive permanent earnings characteristics. Apparently, differences in fixed effects across individuals mostly reflect differences in earnings rather than employment levels.

EMPLOYERS OF LOW EARNERS

Having established the number of characteristics of persistent low earners in the labor market, we now look at their employers. What are the characteristics of the firms that hire low earners? Are they relatively concentrated in particular sectors of the economy, or are they more broadly dispersed? What are their easily observed distinguishing characteristics, such as industry, size, and turnover rates? And to what extent do these firms pay low wages to workers independently of the characteristics of the workers whom they hire?

We shed some light on these questions in tables 3.4 and 3.5. In table 3.4, we analyze the relationship between low earners, on the one hand, and characteristics of firms such as industry, size, and turnover rate, on the other. For each comparison, we present two measures: the distribution of low earners *across* industries or size-turnover categories and the percentage of workers *within* each industry or size-turnover category who had persistently low earnings. The first of these measures gives us some sense of where the greatest number of low earners overall can be found and of how concentrated they are by sector and type of firm. This measure reflects not only the presence of low-wage workers within an industry (or other firm category) but also the relative size of that industry (or firm category). The second measure, in contrast, simply indicates the extent to which any given industry (or firm category) has a higher concentration of low earners, reflecting the average level and/or dispersion of wages in that industry.[8]

Table 3.4 indicates that industries differ quite substantially from one another in the presence of low earners and in the extent to which they account for low earners. From the first column we can see that *the retail trade and service sectors accounted for over three-fourths of all low earners,* with retail trade alone accounting for nearly one-third and eating and drinking establishments accounting for about one-sixth.[9] Of course, this partly reflects the ever-increasing relative size of these sectors as well as their wage levels.[10] But the second column also indicates that, on average, the percentages of workers within these industrial categories who have low earnings are well above the percentages of those found in sectors such as construction, manufacturing, transportation and utilities, and wholesale trade.

Quite importantly, the data in table 3.4 also indicate that there is considerable variation within these broad industry aggregates in the presence of low earners. For instance, while only 4 percent of manufacturing workers were low earners, there were considerably more in nondurable than in durable manufacturing—and especially in the apparel and textile industry, where nearly one-fourth of workers were low earners. Within the low-wage retail trade sector, the presence of low earners in eating and drinking establishments was considerably greater than elsewhere.[11]

As for the services, we find that large percentages of workers in personal services, social services, entertainment (hotels and lodgings), and especially help supply (or "temp") services, had persistently low earnings. In contrast, the health and other business services had low percentages of workers with low earnings. Interestingly, health care and education together account for about one-sixth of all low earners because of the relatively large sizes of these sectors, even though neither is a particularly low-wage sector (as measured by the percentages of workers within each who were low earners). The financial services sector (separate from overall services) is clearly one with only small percentages of low earners by either measure.

What about other easily observable characteristics of firms, such as size and turnover rates? In the lower part of table 3.4, we find that about one-

Table 3.4   Worker Earnings and Distribution of Low Earners Across
            Firm Categories

	Distribution of Low Earners Across Firm Categories	Percentage of Workers in Each Category Who Are Low Earners	Total Annual Earnings
All firms	1.00	0.08	$35,233
By industry			
Construction	0.04	0.06	31,568
Manufacturing	0.11	0.04	37,244
Durable goods	0.03	0.02	39,996
Apparel and other textile	0.03	0.24	20,614
Other nondurable goods	0.08	0.07	33,604
Transportation and utilities	0.03	0.03	40,105
Wholesale trade	0.04	0.04	40,380
Retail trade	0.31	0.17	23,990
Eating and drinking places	0.16	0.31	16,929
Other retail trade	0.15	0.11	26,707
Finance, insurance, and real estate	0.03	0.03	42,294
Services	0.43	0.09	35,338
Hotels and other lodging places	0.03	0.18	19,965
Personal services	0.03	0.23	19,535
Business services	0.09	0.12	32,593
Help supply services	0.04	0.23	19,326
Other business services	0.05	0.09	36,981
Health services	0.06	0.05	38,253
Educational services	0.10	0.10	33,422
Social services	0.03	0.15	20,772
Public administration	0.01	0.02	37,345
By firm size (employees)			
Fewer than 25	0.32	0.12	32,901
26 to 100	0.18	0.08	33,616
101 to 500	0.18	0.07	34,307
501 to 1,000	0.07	0.06	34,414
More than 1,000	0.25	0.05	38,085

(Table continues on p. 37.)

Table 3.4   *Continued*

	Distribution of Low Earners Across Firm Categories	Percentage of Workers in Each Category Who Are Low Earners	Total Annual Earnings
By annual worker turnover			
0 to 10 percent	0.01	0.02	51,777
11 to 25 percent	0.10	0.03	41,111
26 to 50 percent	0.30	0.06	35,977
51 to 100 percent	0.51	0.12	28,477
More than 100 percent	0.08	0.20	28,088

Source: Authors' compilation.
Note: The distribution of low earners across major SIC divisions (one-digit industries) sums up to 1.

third of all low earners could be found in small firms (those with twenty-five or fewer workers) and half could be found in small to medium-sized ones (those with one hundred or fewer workers). This is noteworthy, since the latter categories account for much smaller percentages of nonlow earners.[12] The percentages of workers in each size category who were low earners decline continuously with size.[13] Still, large firms (those with more than one hundred workers) also account for half of all low earners simply by virtue of the fact that they employ large fractions of the overall workforce.

As for turnover rates, we find that low earners were much more heavily concentrated in high-turnover than in low-turnover establishments. Indeed, the percentage of workers with low earnings declines continuously with the turnover rate of the establishment. Of all low earners, nearly 60 percent are found in establishments with annual turnover rates of 50 percent or more each year.

Of course, the turnover rates themselves might well be endogenous with respect to wages (see, for instance, Holzer and Lalonde 2000). In other words, the wages paid at some firms may be limited on account of the high turnover rates of the workers they employ, but turnover rates may also respond to the low wages paid at some firms. Employers make explicit decisions about how much training to provide their workers and the combinations of wages and turnover to accept as a result.[14] Still, the percentages of overall workers at most firms who are low earners are small enough that their wages cannot alone be driving differences across firms in turnover rates; even if the exact pattern of causation is unclear, the strong correlation between low earnings and turnover is noteworthy.

The data in table 3.4 establish quite clearly that the presence of low earners is strongly associated with observable characteristics of firms such as industry, size, and turnover rate. But do some firms pay low wages only because of the lower skills of the workers they hire, or do they pay wage premia (positive or negative) independently of those hired? And to what extent is the presence of low earners in an industry related to the existence of these wage premia?

Some evidence on these questions appears in figure 3.3 and table 3.5. In figure 3.3, we plot the fractions of low earners in firms by quartiles of the firm fixed-effects distribution. The firm fixed effects, as we noted in chapter 2, reflect those permanent characteristics of a firm—such as its capital stock, technology, and human resource policies—associated with higher earnings even after controlling for the workers it employs.[15]

The results of figure 3.3 are quite striking: the vast majority of low earners are found in the bottom quartile of firms according to fixed effects. In other words, *the presence of low earners in a firm seems strongly related to the firm wage premium,* instead of (or perhaps in addition to) being related to low earners' own characteristics. This finding is consistent with the work of John Abowd and others (for example, Abowd and Kramarz 1999) that shows that firm wage premia contribute importantly to overall earnings variation, but it also demonstrates just how strong the correlation is between low earnings status and low firm premia.

Unfortunately, the firm fixed effect is not easily observable to anyone (except for econometricians with access to data such as LEHD). To render this insight useful, we need to relate the firm wage premium to characteristics of firms that are more easily observable, such as those considered in table 3.4. Accordingly, table 3.5 presents the distribution of industries, size, and turnover categories across the four quartiles of the fixed-effects distribution of firms.

The results reported in table 3.5 indicate that some industries are heavily concentrated in the bottom of the firm fixed-effects distribution.[16] These industries include retail trade (especially eating and drinking establishments), some parts of the service sector (such as personal services, help supply, and educational services), and even some parts of manufacturing (apparel and textiles). Of course, these are the same industries in which we find large concentrations of low earners in table 3.4. Thus, once again, the industries that pay low wages to workers are those with low wage premia, not just those that pay low wages because of the characteristics of those they employ. And even within very detailed industries (for example,

Figure 3.3   Fraction of Workers in Each Firm Effect Quartile Who Are Low Earners

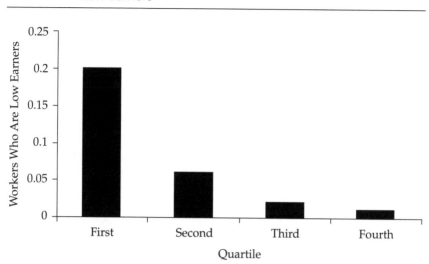

Source: Authors' compilation.

four-digit) there is considerable variation across firms in the wage premia paid to workers and considerable discretion at the firm level in what wages to pay.

Other findings appear in table 3.5 with regard to firm characteristics such as size and turnover rate. The percentages of firms in the bottom quartile of the fixed-effects distribution decline continuously with size and rise very strongly with firm turnover rate. The latter finding suggests that turnover rates respond to establishment characteristics and are not strictly predetermined by the nature of the workers hired.

These findings strongly indicate that a firm's pay policies may contribute importantly to the earnings of its workers, and especially to the presence of low earners. But why do some firms and industries pay more than others, and why do these differences persist? Economists have debated these issues for decades. Some employers—such as those that are unionized—are forced to pay more than others, while others apparently choose to do so either because they believe it ultimately raises productivity and/or lowers costs (for example, by helping them to attract and retain better workers) or because they have non-economic reasons for keeping pay levels low.[17] Whatever the reason, the relationship between firm-level

Table 3.5   Distribution of Employer Characteristics Across Quartiles of
Firm Fixed Effects

	First	Second	Third	Fourth	All
All firms	0.25	0.25	0.25	0.25	1.00
By industry					
Construction	0.19	0.27	0.27	0.27	1.00
Manufacturing	0.09	0.21	0.27	0.42	1.00
Durable goods	0.06	0.19	0.26	0.49	1.00
Apparel and other textile	0.48	0.38	0.12	0.03	1.00
Other nondurable goods	0.14	0.24	0.28	0.34	1.00
Transportation and utilities	0.13	0.19	0.21	0.47	1.00
Wholesale trade	0.12	0.25	0.33	0.30	1.00
Retail trade	0.62	0.24	0.11	0.04	1.00
Eating and drinking places	0.89	0.08	0.03	0.01	1.00
Other retail trade	0.51	0.30	0.14	0.05	1.00
Finance, insurance, and real estate	0.10	0.24	0.35	0.31	1.00
Services	0.30	0.29	0.23	0.18	1.00
Hotels and other lodging places	0.50	0.47	0.03	0.01	1.00
Personal services	0.55	0.26	0.14	0.05	1.00
Business services	0.33	0.23	0.19	0.25	1.00
Help supply services	0.59	0.28	0.09	0.04	1.00
Other business services	0.25	0.21	0.22	0.32	1.00
Health services	0.09	0.28	0.45	0.18	1.00
Educational services	0.52	0.41	0.06	0.01	1.00
Social services	0.38	0.40	0.19	0.04	1.00
Public administration	0.10	0.25	0.45	0.21	1.00
By firm size (employees)					
Fewer than 25	0.36	0.25	0.21	0.19	1.00
26 to 100	0.24	0.28	0.29	0.19	1.00
101 to 500	0.20	0.25	0.29	0.25	1.00
501 to 1,000	0.22	0.24	0.28	0.26	1.00
More than 1,000	0.22	0.24	0.22	0.31	1.00
By annual worker turnover					
Less than 10 percent	0.05	0.03	0.08	0.83	1.00
10 to 25 percent	0.13	0.27	0.31	0.29	1.00
26 to 50 percent	0.23	0.27	0.27	0.23	1.00
51 to 100 percent	0.38	0.24	0.20	0.18	1.00
More than 100 percent	0.46	0.17	0.14	0.23	1.00

Source: Authors' compilation.

pay differences and low earnings has not been strongly emphasized in the literature on poverty and in policy prescriptions for the low-wage labor market—a point to which we return later in this chapter and later in the book.[18]

THE MATCHING OF WORKERS TO FIRMS IN THE LABOR MARKET

The preceding results indicate that firm characteristics and behavior contribute to the earnings of workers independently of the workers' characteristics. But exactly how are workers sorted across (or "matched" to) different kinds of firms? The matching process is a complex one; outcomes represent the intersection between worker preferences and behaviors—in terms of which jobs they apply for—and employer preferences and behavior in recruiting and screening job applicants.

No doubt, the skills of some groups of workers, relative to those sought by employers, play an important role here. But so do other factors. For instance, networks and "connections" in the labor market may steer some demographic groups toward particular employers and sectors of the economy, as may the location of firms relative to worker residences. Indeed, both may ultimately reflect employer choices about where to locate and the groups of workers from whom to seek referrals (see Kirschenman and Neckerman 1991; Moss and Tilly 2001).[19] Discriminatory preferences about whom to hire may certainly play a role as well, as may affirmative action policies in recruitment and hiring for government contractors and others.[20]

In tables 3.6 and 3.7, we provide a bit of additional evidence on the ways in which various demographic subgroups of workers are distributed across firms with different characteristics. In table 3.6, we consider the distribution of race-ethnic and gender groups as well as foreign-born versus native U.S.-born workers across industry, size, and turnover categories—in other words, firm characteristics that are observable in the labor market. In table 3.7, we consider similar distributions of demographic groups across the distribution of firm fixed effects, reflecting the wage premia paid by firms independently of the workers hired.

Table 3.6 indicates a number of interesting patterns in demographic group matching to firms. Not unexpectedly, females were more heavily concentrated than males in the financial and other services, while males were more concentrated in construction, manufacturing, and wholesale trade. Thus, despite the growing presence of females in certain occupations and industries that have been traditionally filled by males, certain differences by gender in sectors of employment persist.

Table 3.6 Distribution of Workers Across Categories of Firm Characteristics, by Demographic Group

	Females				Males				Place of Birth	
	White	Black	Asian	Hispanic	White	Black	Asian	Hispanic	Foreign-Born	U.S.-Born
By industry										
Construction	0.02	0.01	0.01	0.01	0.10	0.06	0.02	0.10	0.04	0.06
Manufacturing	0.13	0.15	0.20	0.23	0.22	0.23	0.27	0.29	0.25	0.18
Transportation and utilities	0.05	0.06	0.04	0.04	0.09	0.10	0.06	0.06	0.05	0.07
Wholesale	0.05	0.02	0.06	0.06	0.09	0.06	0.10	0.09	0.08	0.07
Retail trade	0.15	0.11	0.13	0.14	0.13	0.13	0.17	0.18	0.15	0.14
Finance, insurance, and real estate	0.11	0.09	0.11	0.08	0.06	0.04	0.05	0.03	0.06	0.08
Services	0.46	0.49	0.43	0.41	0.26	0.29	0.30	0.23	0.34	0.36
Public administration	0.04	0.08	0.03	0.04	0.06	0.08	0.03	0.02	0.02	0.06
All	1.00	1.00	1.00	1.00	1.00	1.00	1.00	1.00	1.00	1.00
By firm size (employees)										
Fewer than 25	0.20	0.08	0.19	0.18	0.23	0.12	0.24	0.22	0.22	0.20
26 to 100	0.15	0.11	0.14	0.17	0.19	0.16	0.18	0.24	0.19	0.16
101 to 500	0.19	0.22	0.21	0.23	0.20	0.23	0.21	0.25	0.23	0.20
501 to 1,000	0.09	0.10	0.08	0.08	0.08	0.10	0.07	0.07	0.08	0.09
More than 1,000	0.37	0.50	0.38	0.34	0.31	0.40	0.30	0.21	0.28	0.36
All	1.00	1.00	1.00	1.00	1.00	1.00	1.00	1.00	1.00	1.00
By annual worker turnover										
0 to 10 percent	0.02	0.04	0.04	0.03	0.04	0.04	0.03	0.02	0.03	0.04
11 to 25 percent	0.25	0.23	0.29	0.24	0.23	0.21	0.25	0.19	0.21	0.24
26 to 50 percent	0.40	0.40	0.37	0.38	0.38	0.37	0.37	0.39	0.39	0.39
51 to 100 percent	0.30	0.30	0.27	0.31	0.31	0.34	0.31	0.36	0.34	0.31
More than 100 percent	0.02	0.02	0.03	0.03	0.03	0.03	0.04	0.03	0.04	0.03
All	1.00	1.00	1.00	1.00	1.00	1.00	1.00	1.00	1.00	1.00

Source: Authors' compilation.

But within each gender there are also some noteworthy patterns. For instance, white and Hispanic males were more heavily concentrated in construction than were black males and Asians, while Hispanic and Asian males (especially those who were foreign-born) were more heavily concentrated in manufacturing. Black males were more heavily concentrated in the transportation and utilities and public sectors than were other males. Somewhat similar patterns prevail among women: Hispanics and Asians were heavily concentrated in manufacturing and wholesale trade, while white and black women were more often found in the service and public sectors.

What accounts for these ethnic and racial differences in sectors of employment? Some reflect the long-standing "niches" that particular ethnic groups have established in certain industries, particularly in some regions of the country. Networks often develop that help to maintain these niches over time, particularly if some employers are from the same ethnic group as the workers or employers are pleased with their ethnic workers and encourage them to recruit other coethnics to their firms.[21] At the same time, differences in educational attainment and English-language skills limit the presence of immigrants in some industries and jobs, such as the parts of the retail trade and service sectors that require interaction with customers. And it may also be true that employers discriminate in favor of some groups and against others to accommodate the preferences of customers to be served by members of their own racial-ethnic group.[22]

But the concentration of racial and ethnic groups in different industries also evolves over time. As gaps in educational attainment among native-born groups have diminished and antidiscrimination laws have been implemented, at least some differences in racial distributions across industries have diminished.[23] But other new patterns are less easily accounted for by these factors. For example, the decline in the representation of black men in manufacturing may partly reflect the well-known rise in skills demanded by manufacturers over the past few decades, but this cannot possibly explain their decline relative to Hispanics and Asians.[24] Instead, the relocation of manufacturers to suburban areas as well as to sites in the South and the West, their preferences for Hispanics and Asians over blacks for unskilled jobs, the growing presence of Hispanic and Asian immigrants in the United States over the past few decades, and the strength of informal networks for these groups are all likely to have contributed to the declining presence of black men in manufacturing, which has no doubt fed their overall employment difficulties in recent decades.[25] The role of informal networks and immigration in explaining patterns of employment in construction is probably even more pronounced.[26]

A few other differences across demographic groups are also notewor-

Table 3.7   Distribution of Workers Across Firm Effects, by
              Demographic Group

	First	Second	Third	Fourth	All
All workers	0.25	0.25	0.25	0.25	1.00
By race-ethnicity and gender					
White females	0.30	0.26	0.24	0.20	1.00
Black females	0.24	0.26	0.27	0.23	1.00
Asian females	0.23	0.26	0.27	0.24	1.00
Hispanic females	0.29	0.30	0.24	0.17	1.00
White males	0.21	0.23	0.25	0.31	1.00
Black males	0.23	0.24	0.26	0.27	1.00
Asian males	0.23	0.24	0.25	0.28	1.00
Hispanic males	0.28	0.30	0.25	0.16	1.00
By place of birth					
Foreign-born	0.26	0.28	0.25	0.21	1.00
U.S.-born	0.25	0.25	0.25	0.26	1.00

Source: Authors' compilation.

thy in terms of employer size and turnover rates. Black men and especially black women were quite heavily concentrated in large establishments. Indeed, over 50 percent of the men and 60 percent of the women worked at firms with more than five hundred workers. This probably reflects the less discriminatory hiring practices that blacks faced at such establishments.[27] Although their greater concentration in large establishments no doubt contributes to their average relative wages, the continuing difficulties that blacks face in being hired by small firms may well contribute to their overall difficulties gaining employment that we noted earlier. In contrast, Hispanics were underrepresented in very large firms and overrepresented in small to medium-sized firms; again, the strength of their informal networks is likely to affect their greater access to small firms. We also note that both blacks and Hispanics were more heavily concentrated at high-turnover firms than were whites.

Finally, in table 3.7 we present the distribution of race-ethnic and gender groups as well as foreign-born versus U.S.-born workers across firms by quartile of firm fixed effect. The differences here are not dramatic, but some patterns can still be found. For instance, *white males were the least likely of all groups to work in firms with very low wage premia* (that is, the bottom quartile of the fixed-effects distribution). Minorities and foreign-born workers were more likely to be found at these firms. But somewhat surprisingly, white females were more likely than any other group to be found there as well. The presence of white females in firms that provide part-time opportunities may help account for this result.

Is the higher presence of white males and lower presence of minorities in firms that pay higher wage premia due to the higher skills of the former? This would be the case if firms' primary motivation for paying higher wage premia were to attract better workers and if our person fixed effects did not fully capture their success in doing so. It is also quite possible that part of the correlation between firm fixed effects and gender (especially among whites) reflects high-wage firms' need for full-time employment combined with the lower likelihood of such employment among (mostly female) homemakers.

In some additional regressions we have run, the lower firm wage premia paid to minorities and females remain even after controlling for person fixed effects that probably capture permanent skill differences across workers.[28] These regressions do not resolve the issue of *why* this differential access occurs—especially given the relative paucity of observable personal characteristics (beyond basic demographics and experience) in the LEHD data. But as noted earlier, the race-gender pattern of employment that we observe across industries in table 3.6 cannot be mostly attributed to skill differences; moreover, the large body of literature documented in this chapter (especially in notes 20 to 28) suggests that discrimination, informal networks, and spatial considerations all contribute to these patterns. These factors, in addition to differences in the skills and personal preferences of the workers themselves, no doubt contribute to the earnings outcomes we observe across groups.

CONCLUSIONS

In this chapter, we defined persistently low earners as those prime-age workers earning $12,000 or less in each of at least three years. Not surprisingly, these workers are more likely to be minority, female, foreign-born, and/or younger than those with higher earnings.

But the data clearly indicate that low earners are not randomly distributed across firms. Certain industries (especially retail trade and some of the services), small firms, and firms with high turnover are most likely to employ low earners. These are also the firms that pay low wage premia, independently of the characteristics of the workers they hire. Different demographic groups are also distributed across industries and other categories of firms in systematically different ways; these distributions no doubt reflect a range of factors, including local geography, networks, and the preferences and behaviors of both employers and workers.

Taken together, the results suggest that *the access of minorities and others with fewer skills to firms and sectors that pay high wage premia is limited* and that this limited access may well contribute to their earnings difficulties over time.

In the next chapter, we consider the extent to which low earners improve their earnings over time and the role played by access to higher-wage employers in this process.

Chapter Four | Transitions Out of Low Earnings: Who, When, and Where?

In the previous chapter, we showed that persistently low earners tend to be concentrated not only in certain demographic groups but also in certain kinds of firms. The results suggested that uneven access across groups to employment in high-wage sectors and firms contributes to the consistently low earnings of many workers in the labor market. In this chapter, we focus on *transitions* out of low-earnings status for those workers who earned less than $12,000 per year for at least a three-year period.

A number of important questions arise in such an analysis. For instance, are transitions out of low earnings "partial" (entailing at least some period of earnings under $15,000) or "complete" (entailing consistent earnings above that level)? How frequently does each type of transition occur? To what extent are transitions out of low earnings accompanied by increases in employment (measured by total or full quarters worked) as opposed to earnings per full quarter worked? How important was the boom of the late 1990s to these transitions? Was there any significant impact from policy changes such as the increases in the federal minimum wage implemented in 1996 and 1997?

Beyond these basic facts, we are most interested in *who* made the transition out of low earnings (in terms of demographics and other personal characteristics) and *where* these transitions occurred (in terms of type of firm). Indeed, if low earners are heavily concentrated in particular sectors of the economy and in firms with low wages, we would imagine that *transitions out of low earnings are associated with employment in other sectors and in higher-wage firms.* In fact, this is what we find.

In the previous chapter, we focused on a three-year base period—1993 to 1995—in defining low earners and analyzing their personal characteris-

47

tics and those of their employers. To answer the questions raised in this chapter and shed light on the issues of to whom and where transitions occur, we focus here on the two subsequent periods, 1996 to 1998 and 1999 to 2001. Thus, we focus primarily on individuals who were persistently low earners in the base period and follow them over the subsequent six years.

We consider the personal characteristics of initial low earners who either did or did not transition out of this status by 2001, as well as the characteristics of the employers with whom they made that transition or not. Since some individuals had many employers over this time period, we focus on each individual's primary employer during the 1999 to 2001 period when analyzing the link between employers and earnings outcomes in that period. In the next chapter, we consider the extent to which positive outcomes are associated with *staying* with the same employer over time as opposed to *changing* to a better job. The analysis in chapters 5 and 6 also allows for the possibility that employment outcomes in the final period depended not only on an individual's employer during that time period but also on his or her skills and work experiences obtained with earlier employers.

As in the previous chapter, we present distributions across our earnings categories, supplemented by data on more general (continuous) measures of earnings and employment. Most of the results are once again summary in nature, but we do present some multiple regression analysis toward the end of this chapter that attempts to disentangle the effects of employer characteristics from those of employees and to estimate the relative magnitudes of each. An appendix to the chapter presents some comparable results for subsamples of individuals in the LEHD data who can be matched to CPS surveys. Since the CPS provides us with richer data on the characteristics of individuals (such as educational attainment) and their families (including household income and number of earners), we can determine with greater certainty that our results pertain to less-educated and/or lower-income workers in the low-wage labor market rather than to those who may be choosing low hours and therefore have low earnings voluntarily.

THE KIND AND FREQUENCY OF
TRANSITIONS OUT OF LOW EARNINGS

For those who were persistent low earners over our three-year base period, how frequently did they escape this status in subsequent years? Figure 4.1 presents the distribution of all workers across our four earnings categories in the subsequent periods of 1996 to 1998 and 1999 to 2001. The sample is the same as before—in other words, those with consistent labor

Figure 4.1   Distribution of Workers Across Earnings Categories in 1996 to 1998 and 1999 to 2001

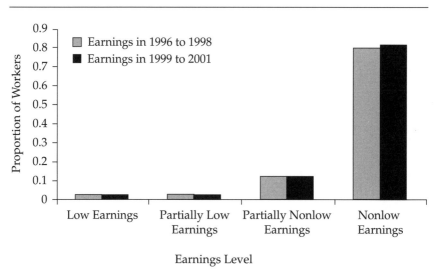

Source: Authors' compilation.

market attachment (at least one quarter per year) who were prime-age workers in 1993.

The results show that fewer workers than in the earlier period—3 to 4 percent compared with nearly 8 percent—were persistently low earners. Also, about 80 percent became nonlow earners, making over $15,000 each year (compared to about two-thirds before). Clearly, this group improved its labor market status with time. The number of workers with partially low or nonlow earnings declined as well, from about 25 percent to 16 percent.

What kinds of transitions generated these outcomes, especially among those who were low earners in the initial period? Table 4.1 presents *transition matrices* across the four earnings categories—one from the 1993 to 1995 period to the 1996 to 1998 period, and the other from the 1993 to 1995 period to the 1999 to 2001 period. Each row in a transition matrix presents the probability of ending up in one of the four earnings categories in the latter period, conditional on being in one of the four categories in the initial period. Each row thus adds up to 100 percent, to indicate what became of all workers in any earnings category in the initial period. Those on the diagonal line (top left to bottom right) are the percentages in each initial category who were subsequently in the same categories as before; those

Table 4.1   Earnings Transition Matrices

	Earnings in 1996 to 1998					Earnings in 1999 to 2001				
	Low	Partially Low	Partially Nonlow	Nonlow	All	Low	Partially Low	Partially Nonlow	Nonlow	All
Earnings in 1993 to 1995										
Low	0.43	0.21	0.28	0.08	1.00	0.29	0.17	0.27	0.27	1.00
Partially low	0.11	0.27	0.41	0.21	1.00	0.09	0.16	0.33	0.42	1.00
Partially nonlow	0.03	0.05	0.28	0.64	1.00	0.03	0.04	0.22	0.71	1.00
Nonlow	0.00	0.00	0.06	0.93	1.00	0.01	0.01	0.08	0.91	1.00

Source: Authors' compilation.
Note: Each row presents the probability that a worker in a certain earnings category in 1993 to 1995 ends up in the given category in a later period.

above the line are the percentages with improved earnings, while those below are those whose earnings deteriorated.

The first matrix shows that *over half of the initial low earners transitioned out of this category in the subsequent three years.* Most of these transitions, however, were into partially low or partially nonlow earnings categories; in other words, these individuals earned above $12,000, and perhaps even above $15,000, but generally not consistently above the latter figure. Indeed, only 8 percent of the initial low earners became consistently nonlow earners with annual earnings above $15,000. At the same time, the earnings of some workers clearly deteriorated over time. Of those with initially nonlow earnings, about 7 percent slipped into partially low or nonlow categories. Some downward slippage out of partially low and nonlow categories (8 percent and 11 percent, respectively) is observed as well.

Over the next three years—1999 to 2001—we find even greater improvements for those with initially low earnings. *Over the entire nine-year period, more than two-thirds of the initial low earners improved their earnings status.* Although the majority of those with improved earnings were still transitioning into partially low or partially nonlow categories, we find that over one-quarter of the initial low earners achieved nonlow status, or earnings consistently above $15,000 a year. Data on transitions between the two subsequent periods (not presented in the table) also indicate some clear sorting of workers over time: a greater fraction of those who initially made partial escapes from low-earner status improved their status again, while those who remained low earners in the middle three years were more likely to remain so in the last three years.[1]

Are the high rates of transition out of low earnings due entirely to the relatively low thresholds that we have established for partial and even complete escapes from low-earner status (discussed in chapter 3)? Table 4.2 presents data on the earnings and employment levels and changes that underlie the observed transitions across categories for initial low earners. In particular, the table presents earnings and employment levels for the last three-year period that can be compared to those (in table 3.2) for the base period, as well as changes in earnings and employment over the entire nine-year period. The results are presented for all who were initially low earners and also separately for those in one of three transition categories (no transition, partial transition, and full transition) in the period 1999 to 2001. Thus, the outcomes associated with each such observed category can now be ascertained.

The results show that *mean earnings more than doubled for all initial low earners over the entire nine-year period.*[2] Annual earnings in the latest period averaged over $15,000, compared with roughly $7,000 for the same workers initially. Similarly, average quarterly earnings rose to over $4,000 from roughly half that amount earlier. Median (as opposed to mean) increases were somewhat smaller—median annual earnings grew by 70 percent, and median quarterly earnings rose to about $3,500.

Still, these results imply quite strong earnings growth for low earners that is not strictly determined by the escape thresholds we have established. The significant improvements in earnings for low earners in this time period have also been observed elsewhere (Connolly, Gottschalk, and Newman 2003).[3] The strong earnings growth may be partly attributable to the aging of this cohort and its gaining of work experience—particularly among those age twenty-five to thirty-four at the outset—as we show later in the chapter. Or it may be due to other unique factors associated with this period, such as the very strong economy. But the overall rates of earnings growth are quite noteworthy.

To what extent do these improvements reflect higher employment rates over time as opposed to higher earnings when working? The data in table 4.2 indicate that growth rates in annual earnings are somewhat higher than those in quarterly or full quarterly earnings, but not dramatically higher. For instance, median quarterly earnings grew by 66 percent over the full period, and median full quarterly earnings grew by 57 percent. Full quarters worked increased to between nine and ten in the last three years, while the number of employers declined somewhat (to a median of one and a mean of two). But the largest growth in annual earnings is clearly generated from improvements in full quarter earnings rather than from quarters worked.

Looking within each of the earnings transition categories in the latter period, we find average earnings and employment levels in each that are not dramatically different from what they were in the base period. Of course, this is to be expected, since each category represents a truncation of earnings according to the same definitions as before. Only those with nonlow earnings show no such truncation at the upper level—and therefore significantly higher average earnings than before. Earnings growth also appears to be fairly evenly split across the two three-year periods that are combined in table 4.2.[4]

Overall, the results show some very substantial earnings growth for initial low earners over time, even though most only partially rather than fully escaped low-earner status.

WHEN DID THE IMPROVEMENTS OCCUR?

One of the first questions that might be asked about these improvements is the extent to which they were generated by two relatively unique factors associated with the late 1990s: the booming economy and the increases in the

Table 4.2   Earnings and Employment in 1999 to 2001 for Initial Low
             Earners

Transition Status in 1999 to 2001	Level		Growth	
	Mean	Median	Mean	Median
Annual earnings				
All	15,846	13,277	1.30	0.76
Still low	7,644	7,780	0.16	0.08
Partial escape	14,008	13,389	0.98	0.74
Full escape	27,450	23,630	3.00	2.24
Quarterly earnings				
All	4,166	3,496	1.09	0.66
Still low	2,110	2,139	0.15	0.08
Partial escape	3,762	3,508	0.87	0.64
Full escape	6,983	5,999	2.44	1.83
Full quarter earnings				
All	4,173	3,527	1.13	0.57
Still low	2,132	2,153	0.17	0.07
Partial escape	3,814	3,510	0.89	0.55
Full escape	6,829	5,884	2.50	1.62
Quarters worked				
All	11.37	12.00	0.57	0.00
Still low	11.04	12.00	0.01	0.00
Partial escape	11.29	12.00	0.45	0.00
Full escape	11.85	12.00	1.34	1.00
Full quarters worked				
All	8.92	10.00	0.55	0.00
Still low	8.55	10.00	−0.67	−1.00
Partial escape	8.52	9.00	0.29	0.00
Full escape	9.96	11.00	2.24	2.00
Number of employers				
All	2.09	1.00	0.55	0.00
Still low	2.01	1.00	−0.67	−1.00
Partial escape	2.32	2.00	0.29	0.00
Full escape	1.80	1.00	2.24	2.00

Source: Authors' compilation.
Note: The transition status of initial low earners is defined as "still low" if earnings in 1999 to 2001 were low; "partial escape" if earnings were partially low or partially nonlow; and "full escape" if earnings were nonlow. "Growth" denotes average earning growth between 1993 to 1995 and 1999 to 2001.

Figure 4.2   Average Quarterly Earnings in 1996 to 2001 for
Workers with Low Earnings in 1993 to 1995

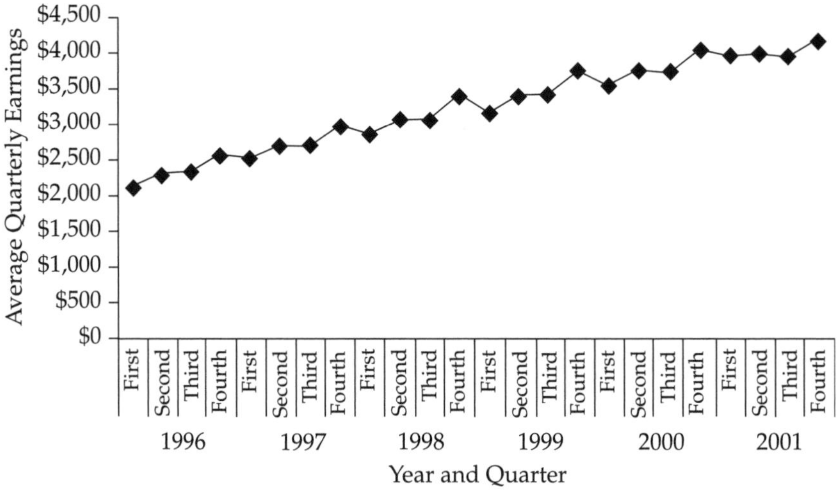

Source: Authors' compilation.

federal minimum wage, implemented in 1996 and 1997, respectively. In particular, the nation's unemployment rate improved from over 7 percent in 1992 to roughly 4 percent in 1999 and 2000 before deteriorating in the recession that began in 2001 (and rising to an average of 5 percent for that year). The federal minimum wage was increased in the fourth quarter of 1996 from $4.25 an hour to $4.75, and then to $5.15 in the fourth quarter of 1997.

A closer look at exactly when various increases in earnings or employment occurred should shed some light on the extent to which these macroeconomic and policy changes were responsible. Figure 4.2 presents data on earnings for those who were initial low earners separately for each quarter in the period 1996 to 2001.[5]

The results show little dramatic variation in the rates of annual earnings increases across different years, despite the ups and downs associated with the business cycle. Annual earnings improvements during the period 1996 to 1998 do not appear any lower than those in the years 1999 to 2001, when the labor markets tightened dramatically. On the other hand, progress in the recession year of 2001 clearly seems more modest. Comparisons across states with different unemployment rates at the peak of the cycle suggest similarly small effects associated with business cycle conditions.[6]

Furthermore, increases in the federal minimum wage between the third and fourth quarters of 1996 and 1997 do not appear to have led to increases in the earnings of initial low earners that were markedly greater than those that occurred between the same quarters in other years. Perhaps the effects of minimum-wage increases are greater for those who are younger than our sample of prime-age earners.[7]

To gain more insight into the role of tight labor markets and minimum-wage increases in generating earnings increases in the late 1990s, we have estimated some additional regressions for the log (quarterly earnings) in which we control for some personal characteristics (such as experience), quarter of the year, and year effects (or dummies). Controlling for year effects enables us to separate out the effects of the very strong economy from other factors, such as the aging of the cohort (which might have generated its greatest effects earlier on when the cohort was relatively younger). In some cases, we interacted the year and quarter dummies to infer whether earnings growth between the third and fourth quarters of 1996 and 1997 exceeded the growth observed between these quarters in other years.

Our results are very consistent with what we observe in figure 4.2. Earnings gains in the period 1995 to 1998 were a bit larger than those in the period 1999 to 2001 and substantially larger than those observed in 2000 to 2001. The ongoing tightening of the economy during the middle to late 1990s seems to have generated greater earnings increases than might otherwise have occurred, though these increases moderated somewhat once the unemployment rate stabilized (at very low levels) at the end of the decade.[8] The emergence of a recession in 2001 dampened this growth considerably. On the other hand, we find little difference in earnings growth between the third and fourth quarters of 1996 and 1997 and the third and fourth quarters of 1997 and 1998 relative to these same quarters in other years.

Overall, the strong economy of the late 1990s appears to have helped generate some earnings improvements for low earners. Considering that the dramatic improvements in earnings for low-income families associated with the Earned Income Tax Credit are not even captured here, the results support the view that this was a period of significant income improvement for low earners.[9]

WHOSE EARNINGS IMPROVED AMONG LOW EARNERS?

Among those who had persistently low earnings in the base period 1993 to 1995, whose earnings improved in the subsequent two periods? In other words, did the transitions out of low earnings and the accompanying improvements in earnings and employment vary greatly across demographic groups? The answer to these questions can shed light on the extent to which such improvements are associated with the personal characteristics of these workers, though any such observed differences may reflect differences in opportunities across groups as well as in their skills and earnings capacity.

In table 4.3, we present the distributions across our earnings categories in the period 1999 to 2001 of those who were initial low earners during 1993 to 1995 separately by age, race-ethnicity and gender, place of birth (foreign-born versus U.S.-born), and quartile of the person fixed-effects distribution. For each subgroup, we also present mean and median growth in annual earnings over this period.

A number of findings appear in the table. For one thing, *transition rates out of low earnings and growth rates in earnings tend to fall considerably with age.* For instance, nearly 35 percent of the youngest age group (twenty-five- to thirty-four-year-olds) had completely escaped into nonlow earnings by the period 1999 to 2001, whereas only 18 percent had done so among those age forty-five to fifty-four. In fact, only about one-fifth of the original low earners in the twenty-five- to thirty-four-year-old age group remained persistently low earners by the final period considered here, whereas over 40 percent of the oldest group remained low earners. Similarly, growth in mean and median earnings was considerably higher for the youngest group than the oldest group.

Of course, this finding is not terribly surprising. It is well known among economists that earnings growth diminishes fairly continuously with age or labor market experience (see, for instance, Mincer 1974). Still, the data indicate that considerable movement out of low earnings occurred for all groups of prime-age low earners, with fewer than half remaining persistently low earners (by our definition) in all age groups.

Comparing across race-ethnic and gender groups, we find that: (1) *males had higher rates of escape out of low earnings, and higher average earnings growth, than females within each race-ethnic group; (2) white males had higher rates of escape and earnings growth than any other group;* and (3) *Asians did better over time than blacks and Hispanics.* Also, U.S.-born workers escaped low earnings more frequently than foreign-born workers and had higher rates of earnings growth.

What accounts for these differences across groups in earnings growth and escape out of low-earnings status over time? It is striking that the pattern of earnings growth differences across groups is similar to the pattern described in chapter 3 for who tends to be concentrated among low earners in the first place—in other words, those groups with the highest earnings and fewest low earners in the base period also tended to have the highest rates of earnings growth, even conditional on being low earners early on.

Table 4.3   Earnings Transitions and Growth Rates, by Demographic
Characteristics for Initial Low Earners

| | Earnings Status in the Period 1999 to 2001 | | | | | Growth in Annual Earnings Between 1993 to 1995 and 1999 to 2001 | |
	Low	Partially Low	Partially Nonlow	Nonlow	All	Mean	Median
All workers	0.28	0.17	0.27	0.27	1.00	1.29	0.76
By race-ethnicity and gender							
White females	0.32	0.17	0.25	0.26	1.00	1.19	0.70
Black females	0.27	0.21	0.29	0.23	1.00	1.03	0.68
Asian females	0.27	0.14	0.26	0.33	1.00	1.45	0.90
Hispanic females	0.31	0.22	0.26	0.21	1.00	0.96	0.61
White males	0.23	0.12	0.29	0.36	1.00	1.90	1.08
Black males	0.24	0.16	0.35	0.25	1.00	1.28	0.86
Asian males	0.31	0.14	0.22	0.33	1.00	1.75	0.97
Hispanic males	0.18	0.16	0.31	0.34	1.00	1.39	0.93
By age							
25 to 34	0.20	0.15	0.30	0.34	1.00	1.63	1.04
35 to 44	0.29	0.18	0.27	0.26	1.00	1.21	0.73
45 to 54	0.41	0.19	0.22	0.18	1.00	0.88	0.45
By place of birth							
Foreign-born	0.29	0.19	0.26	0.26	1.00	1.17	0.71
U.S.-born	0.28	0.17	0.27	0.28	1.00	1.33	0.78
By person fixed effect (quartile)							
First	0.36	0.19	0.25	0.20	1.00	1.00	0.59
Second	0.20	0.16	0.31	0.33	1.00	1.43	0.93
Third	0.15	0.13	0.29	0.43	1.00	1.94	1.30
Fourth	0.14	0.08	0.27	0.51	1.00	2.86	1.84

Source: Authors' compilation.

The fact that the patterns across groups in earnings *growth* parallel those in transitions out of low-earnings categories suggests that the latter did not simply reflect the fact that some groups are initially closer to the category cutoffs than others (by having higher earnings in the base period); the differences in transition rates accurately reflect differences in growth, not arbitrarily drawn lines. But whether and to what extent their better growth reflects higher initial skills, better access to on-the-job training, better access to high-wage employers, or less discrimination along other dimensions cannot yet be ascertained. We return to these issues later when we try to disentangle these various effects through multiple regression analysis.

One more finding appears in table 4.3: *escapes out of low earnings and rates of earnings growth were higher for those with higher person fixed effects,* perhaps reflecting their higher skills and earnings capacity. In fact, complete rates of escape out of low earnings occurred more than twice as frequently in the highest quartile of the fixed-effects distribution as in the lowest.

It is noteworthy that these results are for the period 1999 to 2001, while fixed effects are estimated over the period ending in 1998; thus, these results do not directly reflect the endogeneity of the fixed effects with respect to earnings in the earlier period. Our ability to disentangle person fixed effects from earnings growth is not completely clean, but our attempt to do so does suggest that skills and perhaps other fixed personal characteristics remain important determinants of who progresses out of low earnings over time.[10]

IN WHAT KINDS OF FIRMS DO WORKERS ESCAPE LOW EARNINGS?

Although it is clear that earnings growth and rates of transition out of low earnings varied with the personal characteristics of the initial low earners, did the *firms* at which these individuals worked also affect their progress over time? Did some workers have more difficulty transitioning out of low earnings because they had less access to high-wage sectors and firms?

In table 4.4, we present the distribution of those who initially had persistently low earnings across different kinds of firms in the period 1999 to 2001, both overall and according to whether they had transitioned out of low earnings. The table presents these results by industry and by size and turnover categories of firms. The table is thus similar in nature to table 3.4, except that it reflects outcomes for a subsequent time period rather than the base period.

One clear finding in the table is that, overall, the *initial low earners*

Table 4.4   Firm Characteristics, by Earnings Transition Categories in
1999 to 2001 for Initial Low Earners

	All	Still Low	Partial Escape	Full Escape
All firms	1.00	1.00	1.00	1.00
By industry				
Construction	0.04	0.02	0.04	0.05
Manufacturing	0.12	0.09	0.13	0.13
Durable goods	0.05	0.02	0.06	0.07
Apparel and other textile	0.02	0.03	0.02	0.00
Other nondurable goods	0.07	0.07	0.07	0.06
Transportation and utilities	0.03	0.02	0.03	0.05
Wholesale trade	0.04	0.03	0.04	0.06
Retail trade	0.24	0.31	0.25	0.16
Eating and drinking places	0.11	0.17	0.10	0.05
Other retail trade	0.13	0.14	0.14	0.11
Finance, insurance, and real estate	0.04	0.02	0.04	0.06
Services	0.47	0.48	0.47	0.45
Hotels and other lodging places	0.02	0.03	0.03	0.02
Personal services	0.02	0.03	0.02	0.01
Business services	0.07	0.07	0.08	0.06
Help supply services	0.03	0.04	0.04	0.02
Other business services	0.04	0.03	0.04	0.04
Health services	0.08	0.06	0.09	0.10
Educational services	0.15	0.18	0.14	0.15
Social services	0.03	0.03	0.04	0.03
Public administration	0.02	0.02	0.02	0.04
By firm size (employees)				
Fewer than 25	0.24	0.33	0.22	0.18
25 to 100	0.16	0.14	0.17	0.16
101 to 500	0.19	0.16	0.21	0.21
501 to 1,000	0.08	0.07	0.08	0.10
More than 1,000	0.33	0.30	0.32	0.36
By annual worker turnover				
Less than 10 percent	0.02	0.04	0.01	0.01
10 to 25 percent	0.19	0.18	0.17	0.25
26 to 50 percent	0.40	0.37	0.39	0.44
51 to 100 percent	0.36	0.37	0.40	0.28
More than 100 percent	0.03	0.04	0.03	0.01

Source: Authors' compilation.
Note: The columns sum to 1 separately for industry, firm size, and turnover categories.

worked for higher-wage industries, larger firms, and firms with lower turnover in the later period than they did earlier on. Comparing the first column of table 4.4 with comparable estimates from table 3.4 shows that substantially fewer of these workers were in retail trade and that somewhat fewer were in the service industries; instead, more now worked in industries such as manufacturing, transportation, and wholesale trade. Only about 40 percent of them worked in firms of fewer than one hundred workers in the later period, in contrast to about half in the earlier period, and fewer than 40 percent now worked in firms with turnover rates of 50 percent or higher (as opposed to nearly 60 percent earlier on).

Furthermore, it is clear that transitions out of low earnings for initial low earners are strongly correlated with the characteristics of the firms for which they worked in the later period. We can infer the association of firm characteristics with transitions by comparing across columns in table 4.4, since each column gives us the distribution of these workers across firm characteristics according to their transition status.

For example, we see in the upper part of the table that *those who were completely escaping low earnings were much more heavily concentrated in construction, manufacturing, transportation and utilities, and wholesale trade than were those who were still persistently low earners.* Those who were "partially escaping" were also more concentrated in these industries than were those who remained low earners, but less concentrated than the "complete escapers." Within one-digit industries, we also see some important distinctions. For example, those escaping low earnings were much more concentrated in durable than nondurable manufacturing and especially textiles and garments; they were less concentrated in eating and drinking establishments than in other parts of the retail trade sector; and they were less concentrated in personal services and temporary agencies than in other parts of the service sector.

In the bottom rows of table 4.4, we similarly find that *those transitioning out of low earnings were much less likely to be concentrated in small firms in the later period (especially those with fewer than twenty-five workers) than those who remained low earners.* They were also less likely to be found in high-turnover establishments than those who remained low earners.

Perhaps the most striking evidence of the relationship between transitions out of low earnings and the characteristics of employers in the subsequent period can be found in figure 4.3. Here we plot the distributions of initial low earners across quartiles of the firm fixed-effects distribution, which, as we noted earlier, reflects firm-level wage premia independently of the characteristics of a firm's employees. We also plot the distributions of these workers across the firm fixed-effects categories according to

Figure 4.3   Earnings Transitions of Initial Low Earners by Quartile of
            Firm Fixed Effect in 1999 to 2001

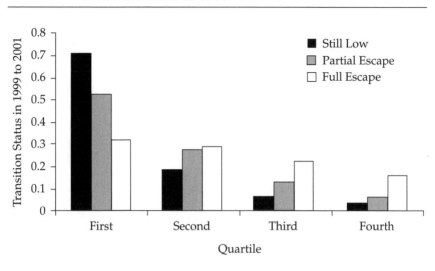

Source: Authors' compilation.

whether they have remained low earners or have partially or completely escaped this status.

The results show that the correlations between firm fixed effect in the later period and transitions out of low earnings are very large. In particular, we find that *nearly three-quarters of those who remained low earners were still in the bottom quartile of firms in terms of their wage premia, while fewer than one-third of those who had completely escaped low-earnings status worked for low-wage firms.* And among those who had partially escaped low earnings, about half worked for low-wage firms. Looking at other quartiles of the firm wage premium distribution, we see much greater relative concentrations of those who escaped low earnings (relative to those who did not) than we find in the bottom quartile.

Of course, these patterns are similar to what we found in chapter 3 regarding the correlations between firm characteristics and low earnings in the base period. The results of this chapter reinforce the earlier results by showing that the ability of persistently low earners to improve their earnings over time seems strongly related to their ability to gain employment in higher-wage sectors or firms.

Later in this chapter we explore the extent to which firm characteristics, as opposed to personal characteristics, determine these better outcomes. The extent to which those who had better jobs and thus escaped low-earnings status stayed in these firms over time or had to change firms and jobs to find such jobs is explored in detail in chapter 5.

Before moving to those results, it is worth presenting a bit more evidence on how the relationships between transitions out of low earnings and firm characteristics vary by race-ethnicity as well as gender. Table 4.5 presents the distribution of these groups across one-digit industries separately for "partial escapers" and "complete escapers" out of initial low-earnings status. These data also are provided for foreign-born versus U.S.-born workers.

A number of findings emerge here. First, *the majority of workers, both male and female, who escaped low earnings did so through the retail trade and service sectors,* even though these are not high-wage sectors. The vast majority of women—generally 70 to 80 percent—who completely escaped low earnings did so through these sectors, while this was less true for men (55 to 65 percent). Black and white women were the ones most likely to escape low earnings through the service and financial industries, while Asian and Hispanic women were more likely to transition through manufacturing than were white or black women. Manufacturing was also a relatively important route out of low earnings for Asian and Hispanic men, as was construction for Hispanic and white men. Black men escaped low earnings more frequently than any other group through transportation and utilities.

Of course, most of these findings parallel what we found in chapter 3. In other words, these happen to be the sectors where each group is relatively most frequently employed rather than the ones where these groups do well relative to other groups also employed in them. For instance, Asian men (and women) were more likely than any other group to transition out of low earnings through retail trade. Yet much larger percentages of these groups who were still low earners were also concentrated in these same sectors.[11]

But in a few notable cases certain groups did relatively well in a particular sector despite their relatively low representation there. For instance, *black males escaped low earnings (partially or completely) through manufacturing more than white males, even though they were less likely to gain such employment.*[12]

What these findings imply is that there is no single path to higher earnings for low earners. Some low-earning groups (especially women) frequently end up advancing in the retail trade and service sectors, even though these are not high-wage sectors overall; others (especially men) are relatively more dependent on the traditional high-wage sectors for advancement. Within any of these sectors there are higher- and lower-wage firms and jobs, and for any group the sectors where they are most frequently employed provide opportunities for advancement. On the other hand, improving the access of some groups to some sectors—like black men to jobs in construction and manufacturing—would probably improve their overall access to good jobs and thus improve their prospects of advancing out of low earnings.

DISENTANGLING PERSON AND FIRM EFFECTS: MULTIPLE REGRESSIONS

These data suggest that both person and firm characteristics contribute importantly to the ability of low earners to transition into higher-earning jobs. But what are the relative magnitudes of each set of contributions? Also, can we account for some differences by race and gender in the rates of transition through their differential access to better firms and jobs?

To answer these questions we provide some multiple regression estimates. In table 4.6, we provide estimates of the effects of person and firm characteristics (in the form of odds ratios from logit regressions) on the probability that any individual with low earnings in the base period will have transitioned completely out of this status by the period 1999 to 2001, while in table 4.7 we present similar results for those who transitioned either partly or completely.[13] In table 4.8, we provide similar estimates for the determinants of ln(average annual earnings) among initially low earners in that period. The models in all cases include observations only for 1999 to 2001, but for each worker who initially had low earnings in the base period; all firm characteristics included thus represent those of the primary employer in that period.[14]

A number of different models are presented in each table. The first model includes only personal characteristics—such as race-gender, place of birth, and potential experience (based largely on age and not included in the table)—as determinants of earnings status. The second is similar, but it replaces race-gender and place of birth with the person fixed effects.[15] We then add observable firm characteristics—industry, size, and turnover—to those two models in the third and fourth equations, while we replace the observable firm characteristics with firm fixed effects in the fifth and sixth equations.[16]

A number of noteworthy findings appear in each table. First, personal characteristics have important effects on our ability to explain transitions out of low earnings and earnings levels more generally in each model. Indeed, both race-gender and person fixed effects have significant effects in all equations. The race-gender effects are consistent with those observed

Table 4.5   Distribution of Initial Low Earners Across Industries in the 1999 to 2001 Period, by Race, Gender, and Place of Birth: Partial and Complete Escapers

	Construction	Manufacturing	Transportation and Utilities	Wholesale	Retail	Finance, Insurance, and Real Estate	Services	Public Administration	All
Partial escapers									
By race-ethnicity and gender									
White females	0.02	0.08	0.02	0.03	0.27	0.05	0.52	0.02	1.00
Black females	0.01	0.10	0.03	0.02	0.18	0.03	0.62	0.02	1.00
Asian females	0.00	0.18	0.02	0.05	0.32	0.05	0.37	0.01	1.00
Hispanic females	0.01	0.25	0.02	0.05	0.18	0.03	0.46	0.01	1.00
White males	0.12	0.11	0.05	0.05	0.25	0.03	0.37	0.02	1.00
Black males	0.09	0.14	0.07	0.05	0.22	0.03	0.38	0.03	1.00
Asian males	0.03	0.15	0.04	0.08	0.40	0.02	0.28	0.00	1.00
Hispanic males	0.10	0.25	0.03	0.07	0.26	0.02	0.27	0.01	1.00
By place of birth									
Foreign-born	0.04	0.23	0.02	0.05	0.25	0.03	0.37	0.01	1.00
U.S.-born	0.04	0.09	0.03	0.03	0.24	0.04	0.50	0.02	1.00

Complete escapers								
By race-ethnicity and gender								
White females	0.02	0.08	0.04	0.05	0.17	0.08	0.52	0.04	1.00
Black females	0.00	0.13	0.04	0.04	0.11	0.07	0.53	0.08	1.00
Asian females	0.01	0.18	0.03	0.05	0.21	0.08	0.41	0.02	1.00
Hispanic females	0.01	0.18	0.04	0.06	0.14	0.05	0.50	0.02	1.00
White males	0.10	0.13	0.07	0.08	0.17	0.05	0.37	0.04	1.00
Black males	0.07	0.17	0.10	0.08	0.16	0.04	0.33	0.05	1.00
Asian males	0.02	0.20	0.06	0.08	0.22	0.05	0.35	0.02	1.00
Hispanic males	0.15	0.24	0.06	0.10	0.18	0.02	0.24	0.02	1.00
By place of birth								
Foreign-born	0.06	0.20	0.04	0.07	0.19	0.05	0.36	0.02	1.00
U.S.-born	0.05	0.11	0.05	0.06	0.15	0.07	0.47	0.05	1.00

Source: Authors' compilation.

Table 4.6   Odds Ratio Estimates of Probability of Fully Escaping Low Earnings in the Period 1999 to 2001

	(1)	(2)	(3)	(4)	(5)	(6)
By race-ethnicity and gender (versus white males)						
White females	0.711**		0.664**		0.714**	
Black females	0.535**		0.479**		0.486**	
Asian females	1.069		1.031		1.060	
Hispanic females	0.520**		0.444**		0.495**	
Black males	0.557**		0.520**		0.546**	
Asian males	1.062		1.173		1.176	
Hispanic males	0.950		0.895*		0.945	
By place of birth (versus U.S.-born)						
Foreign-born	0.849**		0.899**		0.828**	
Person fixed effect		2.556**		3.171**		3.879**
By industry (versus manufacturing)						
Construction			1.581**	1.918**		
Transportation and utilities			1.600**	1.763**		
Wholesale trade			1.614**	1.764**		
Retail trade			0.622**	0.680**		
Finance, insurance, and real estate			2.074**	2.119**		
Services			0.933*	1.009		
Public administration			1.713**	1.923**		
By firm size (versus fewer than 25)						
26 to 100			1.305**	1.283**		
101 to 500			1.485**	1.416**		
501 to 1,000			1.714**	1.644**		
More than 1,000			1.611**	1.563**		
By annual worker turnover (versus less than 10 percent)						
10 to 25 percent			2.172**	2.758**		
26 to 50 percent			1.790**	1.931**		

(Table continues on p. 67.)

Table 4.6   *Continued*

	(1)	(2)	(3)	(4)	(5)	(6)
51 to 100 percent			1.144	1.033		
More than 100 percent			0.623**	0.514**		
Firm fixed effect					6.518**	8.654**

Source: Authors' compilation.
Notes: Each specification is based on 58,792 observations. In addition to reported variables, all specifications include a constant and controls for experience. The odds ratio is the exponential of the estimated coefficient and indicates how the odds of the event change as the variable is changed from 0 to 1. For instance, the odds ratio for black males of 0.557 in column 1 indicates that the odds that black males will fully escape low earnings are little more than half of the odds that white males (the reference category) will fully escape low earnings.
*significant at 5 percent; **significant at 1 percent

in earlier tables: white males enjoy higher earnings and higher rates of transition out of low-earnings status than most other groups.

At the same time, the inclusion of firm characteristics—especially the firm fixed effect—dramatically improves our ability to explain transitions and earnings more generally. In fact, the explanatory power of the ln(earnings) equations in table 4.8 improves significantly when we add firm characteristics to the models, and they more than double when firm fixed effects are included. Differences in transition rates and in earnings levels across industries, firm size categories, and turnover categories are also consistent with what we observed earlier: transitions and earnings are highest in industries such as construction, manufacturing, and transportation and utilities, in the largest firms, and in those with the lowest turnover.

Overall, the results confirm that both personal skills (as measured by the person fixed effects) and race-gender contribute to the probabilities of escaping low earnings. That white males are generally more likely than members of other race-gender groups to escape low earnings is quite remarkable given that so many fewer of them were present among low earners in the first place (as we noted in chapter 3). This implies that those white males who were initially "selected" into this category were relatively lower in their group's distributions of skills and other personal qualities than were those from other race-gender groups.

Still, we cannot attribute this differential with certainty to discrimination, since the regressions do not include both race-gender measures and person fixed effects at the same time (see note 15). The preferences of women for part-time employment might also help to account for their continued lower rates of earnings growth and escape from low earnings (especially among whites). Furthermore, it is not clear that other barriers

Table 4.7 Odds Ratio Estimates of Probability of Fully or Partially Escaping Low Earnings in the Period 1999 to 2001

	(1)	(2)	(3)	(4)	(5)	(6)
By race-ethnicity and gender (versus white males)						
White females	0.648**		0.653**		0.643**	
Black females	0.583**		0.542**		0.495**	
Asian females	0.969		1.011		0.973	
Hispanic females	0.531**		0.485**		0.475**	
Black males	0.742**		0.680**		0.710**	
Asian males	0.825*		0.972		0.916	
Hispanic males	1.063		1.006		1.049	
By place of birth (versus U.S.-born)						
Foreign-born	0.820**		0.858**		0.786**	
Person fixed effect		2.323**		2.670**		3.929**
By industry (versus manufacturing)						
Construction			1.896**	2.450**		
Transportation and utilities			1.581**	1.772**		
Wholesale trade			1.505**	1.655**		
Retail trade			0.548**	0.613**		
Finance, insurance, and real estate			2.014**	2.051**		
Services			0.843**	0.935*		
Public administration			1.540**	1.803**		
By firm size (versus fewer than 25)						
26 to 100			1.370**	1.302**		
101 to 500			1.591**	1.472**		
501 to 1,000			1.858**	1.724**		
More than 1,000			1.701**	1.632**		
By annual worker turnover (versus less than 10 percent)						
10 to 25 percent			1.975**	2.378**		
26 to 50 percent			1.992**	1.927**		
51 to 100 percent			1.690**	1.277**		

(Table continues on p. 69.)

Table 4.7   *Continued*

	(1)	(2)	(3)	(4)	(5)	(6)
More than 100 percent			1.261*	0.845		
Firm fixed effect					6.800**	10.188**

Source: Authors' compilation.
Notes: Each specification is based on 58,792 observations. In addition to reported variables, all specifications include a constant and controls for experience.
*significant at 5 percent; **significant at 1 percent

to access to good jobs explain these patterns, since controlling for job characteristics does not seem to change the observed race-gender differentials in escape rates or earnings growth of the first few estimated models very much.

On the other hand, the patterns of employment differences by racial groups across industries for those escaping low earnings—especially among men—do not appear to match a story based only on unobserved earnings differences. And as we noted in chapter 3, a large body of literature continues to provide strong evidence for the notion that discrimination and other barriers limit the access of minorities to employment at certain kinds of firms and to certain jobs within firms. Thus, it seems unlikely that the greater advances observed among white men can be due entirely to their greater skills, especially given the more negative selection process that landed them among these low earners in the first place.

Our regressions clearly confirm that access to high-wage firms, independently of the characteristics of the workers themselves, has important effects on the ability of low earners to improve their earnings status in subsequent periods. As we noted earlier, perhaps the individuals who gain employment in higher-wage firms have stronger personal characteristics in ways that are not captured by the person fixed effects we attribute to them, or perhaps those who succeed are not really our most disadvantaged workers in the first place.

We explore these issues somewhat in the appendix to this chapter by considering a subsample of our data that is matched to the CPS and for whom more information on personal and family characteristics is available. The results presented there show that transition rates out of low earnings for high school dropouts and those from poor families are indeed somewhat lower than those presented in this chapter. They largely confirm our findings, however, that the characteristics of the firm that employs them matter a great deal for the labor market advancement of disadvantaged low earners.

Table 4.8   Determinants of Log of Total Annual Earnings in the Period
1999 to 2001

	(1)	(2)	(3)	(4)	(5)	(6)
By race-ethnicity and gender (versus white males)						
White females	−0.145**		−0.151**		−0.134**	
Black females	−0.191**		−0.213**		−0.215**	
Asian females	−0.047**		−0.048**		−0.049**	
Hispanic females	−0.196**		−0.225**		−0.210**	
Black males	−0.169**		−0.187**		−0.169**	
Asian males	−0.041*		−0.003		−0.013	
Hispanic males	−0.036**		−0.054**		−0.042**	
By place of birth (versus U.S.-born)						
Foreign-born	−0.033**		−0.014*		−0.034**	
Person fixed effect		0.309**		0.348**		0.415**
By industry (versus manufacturing)						
Construction			0.154**	0.206**		
Transportation and utilities			0.145**	0.166**		
Wholesale trade			0.099**	0.124**		
Retail trade			−0.138**	−0.136**		
Finance, insurance, and real estate			0.195**	0.193**		
Services			−0.027**	−0.016*		
Public administration			0.110**	0.143**		
By firm size (versus fewer than 25)						
26 to 100			0.100**	0.098**		
101 to 500			0.134**	0.126**		
501 to 1,000			0.156**	0.15**		
More than 1,000			0.152**	0.148**		
By annual worker turnover (versus less than 10 percent)						
10 to 25 percent			0.241**	0.296**		
26 to 50 percent			0.198**	0.227**		
51 to 100 percent			0.122**	0.131**		
More than 100 percent			−0.028	−0.016		
Firm fixed effect					0.459**	0.564**

(Table continues on p. 71.)

Table 4.8   *Continued*

	(1)	(2)	(3)	(4)	(5)	(6)
Observations	58,792	58,488	58,753	58,449	55,993	55,717
R-squared	0.06	0.12	0.12	0.19	0.16	0.26

Source: Authors' compilation.
Notes: Each specification is based on 58,792 observations. In addition to reported variables, all specifications include a constant and controls for experience.
*significant at 5 percent; **significant at 1 percent

CONCLUSIONS

In this chapter, we have reviewed the tendency of workers who were persistent low earners in the base period (1993 to 1995) to transition out of this status during the six subsequent years (1996 to 2001). We have also considered the extent to which both personal and firm characteristics in the subsequent periods contributed to transitions out of low earnings for these workers and to earnings levels more generally.

Our results indicate that large fractions of workers who had persistently low earnings in the base period at least partially escaped that status in the subsequent six years, though relatively few transitioned completely out of low earnings. In other words, many workers who never earned above $12,000 in the base period earned more than $12,000 or even more than $15,000 in the subsequent years, though most did not consistently earn above $15,000. Median earnings growth rates of 70 percent for these workers confirm the view that real earnings growth for the initially low earners was substantial. Our summary data suggest that the normal aging process for these workers contributed significantly to these outcomes, as did the strong economy of that period to a lesser extent.

The results also indicate that personal characteristics—such as race-ethnicity, gender, place of birth, person fixed effect, and age—all significantly affect the likelihood that a low earner will transition out of this status over time. At the same time, the firm for which an individual subsequently works contributes importantly as well, independent of the individual's characteristics. The same firm characteristics that are correlated with the tendency for a worker to have low earnings in the base period (chapter 3)—industry, size, turnover rate, and especially the firm wage premium—all have effects on these workers' transitions out of low earnings in the subsequent period as well. The fact that, on average, these individuals worked for better firms over time along these dimensions contributes importantly to the successes that we observe for them over time. Differential access to high-wage firms also accounts for at least some of the differences that we observe in earnings and transition rates across race-ethnic and gender groups.

In the appendix, we consider the extent to which transitions out of low-earnings status and earnings are better served by staying on the same job and accumulating experience and seniority, as opposed to seeking better jobs. The role of the geographic location of workers and firms will also be considered. For now, it seems quite clear that the access of low earners to employment in high-wage firms has an important effect on their prospects for future economic success.

APPENDIX: SAMPLES MATCHED TO THE CURRENT POPULATION SURVEY

As we noted in chapter 3, there are some major limitations to our defini-tions of low earners using the LEHD data. Specifically, we cannot distin-guish those workers who are choosing to consistently work few *hours* (that is, part-time) from those whose earnings are low owing to low *wages* (even as full-time workers). Similarly, we cannot distinguish those who are sec-ond earners in their families from those who are primary breadwinners, and thus we cannot really distinguish those with low earnings from those with low *family incomes.* Also, without demographic characteristics on in-dividuals, such as education, we have no direct evidence on the skill con-straints that individuals face in trying to achieve higher earnings.

Fortunately, the UI wage records in the LEHD data have been matched to a variety of household and economic censuses, including the March Current Population Survey (CPS). Using these data, we can test whether the results we have presented so far—on the frequency of transitions out of low earnings and the role of employer characteristics in generating them—hold for subsamples of low earners who have low education or low family incomes according to data available in the CPS.

We have constructed a sample of individuals who are observed in the CPS up to or during the base period—in other words, individuals who are observed in any year up to 1995.[17] Ideally, we would prefer to have matches on individuals who are observed in the CPS only during the base period, but the sample sizes of the CPS are too small to generate sufficient numbers of matches that way.[18] Alternatively, we would prefer to focus on individual or family traits that do not vary over time. For example, years of educational attainment is a relatively fixed characteristic among prime-age workers, so we are comfortable using matches on this variable that are not the same years as our base period. Unfortunately, this is less true for other measures we consider, such as family income and wages earned.

Table 4A.1   CPS Characteristics of Workers, by Earnings Categories

	Low Earnings	Partially Low Earnings	Partially Nonlow Earnings	Nonlow Earnings	All
Education					
High school dropout	0.28	0.28	0.17	0.09	0.13
High school graduate	0.37	0.33	0.36	0.27	0.30
Some college, no degree	0.15	0.21	0.20	0.21	0.20
College degree	0.20	0.18	0.28	0.43	0.37
All	1.00	1.00	1.00	1.00	1.00
Family income as percentage of poverty level					
Less than 100 percent	0.20	0.17	0.08	0.02	0.05
101 to 200 percent	0.38	0.41	0.38	0.17	0.24
More than 200 percent	0.42	0.43	0.53	0.81	0.71
All	1.00	1.00	1.00	1.00	1.00
Hourly wages					
Less than $8.00	0.73	0.75	0.54	0.13	0.26
$8.00 to $10.00	0.14	0.17	0.20	0.17	0.17
More than $10.00	0.13	0.08	0.26	0.71	0.57
All	1.00	1.00	1.00	1.00	1.00

Source: Authors' compilation.

Nevertheless, having at least one observation on these characteristics gives us some useful information on the relative hardships these individuals face.[19]

Table 4A.1 presents data on the educational attainments, family incomes, and hourly wages observed among workers in our matched CPS subsample, according to their earning status in the base period (1993 to 1995).[20] The results clearly indicate that all of these characteristics are strongly and positively correlated with our measures of individual earnings derived from the LEHD data. But on the issue of whether or not our samples of low earners are disadvantaged, the results are somewhat more mixed.

For example, the data show that most of our persistently low earners in the base period (about 65 percent) had a high school degree or less education. Somewhat surprisingly, nearly 20 percent were college graduates. In terms of family income, only about one-fifth of our low earners had incomes below the poverty line, though most had incomes below twice the poverty line. On the other hand, hourly wages for these workers were consistently low—nearly three-fourths were earning $8.00 per hour or less when observed, and nearly 90 percent were working for $10.00 or less.

Thus, most of the persistently low earners in our sample can be described as individuals with relatively low levels of educational attainment, family incomes, and wages. Still, given the significant fractions of low earners who do not fit into these categories, the data in table 4A.1 might raise some doubts about whether or not our administrative data have been useful in identifying the kinds of low earners about whom we most care in terms of public policy.

But a much more important issue is whether or not our findings about transitions out of low earnings, and the means of achieving them, hold for the subsamples of low-earning individuals in our sample whom the CPS can identify as having low educational attainment and low family incomes. Therefore, in table 4A.2, we present transition rates out of low earnings, in 1996 to 1998 and in 1999 to 2001, for particular subsamples of our initial low earners. The groups we now consider are high school dropouts and/or high school graduates; those in families with income below the poverty line or below 200 percent of the poverty line; and those with wages below $8.00 per hour.

Overall, the transition rates that appear in the table are somewhat lower in magnitude than those presented in table 4.1 for all persistently low earners in the base period. In that table, over 70 percent of the initial low earners transitioned partially or completely out of this status during the subsequent six years, and over one-fourth did so completely. In table 4A.2, the percentages transitioning partially or completely are similar for those below the poverty line (or below 200 percent of the poverty line) but are lower for high school dropouts and those earning low wages (at 56 percent and 54 percent, respectively). Those making full transitions in these groups range from 14 percent to 23 percent. Thus, transition rates for those workers who are disadvantaged are somewhat lower than the rates presented elsewhere in this chapter, though not dramatically so; one might infer that transition rates for those facing the most serious barriers (such as physical or mental health problems or very poor skills and work experience) are lower still.

Among those who make this transition, how important is it to work for a firm with a relatively high wage premium? In table 4A.3, we present data on the means of firm fixed effects for primary employers of the same subsamples of initially low earners that we considered in the previous table. We present these results for the base period and also for the two sub-

Table 4A.2   Earnings Transitions in the Period 1996 to 1998 and the Period 1999 to 2001 for Initial Low Earners, by CPS Characteristics

	Low Earnings	Partially Low Earnings	Partially Nonlow Earnings	Nonlow Earnings	All
Earnings status in 1996 to 1998					
High school dropouts	0.63	0.14	18.37	0.04	1.00
High school dropouts and graduates	0.53	0.20	23.32	0.04	1.00
Family income below poverty level	0.45	0.27	23.94	0.04	1.00
Family income less than 200 percent of poverty level	0.50	0.21	25.56	0.04	1.00
Wages less than $8.00 per hour	0.50	0.28	19.57	0.02	1.00
Earnings status in 1999 to 2001					
High school dropouts	0.44	0.19	0.20	0.17	1.00
High school dropouts and graduates	0.35	0.22	0.22	0.21	1.00
Family income below poverty level	0.30	0.18	0.37	0.15	1.00
Family income less than 200 percent of poverty level	0.29	0.23	0.24	0.23	1.00
Wages less than $8.00 per hour	0.46	0.22	0.19	0.14	1.00

Source: Authors' compilation.

sequent periods, both overall and separately for those who are still low earners and those who have partially or completely transitioned out of low-earnings status.

The data in table 4A.3 clearly show, as before, that the tendency to transition out of low earnings is highly correlated with an individual's ability to gain employment in a high-earnings firm. In other words, those who remained low earners in the subsequent period continued to work for firms with low earnings premia; those who made partial escapes were some-

Table 4A.3 Mean Firm Effect in Base and Subsequent Periods by Earnings Status in Subsequent Period for Inital Low Earners, by CPS Characteristics

| | Earnings Status in Subsequent Period | | | | | | | |
	Low		Partially Low		Partially Nonlow		Nonlow	
Period	1993 to 1995	1996 to 1998	1993 to 1995	1996 to 1998	1993 to 1995	1996 to 1998	1993 to 1995	1996 to 1998
High school dropouts	-0.37	-0.34	-0.23	-0.21	-0.36	-0.06	-0.63	0.24
High school dropouts and graduates	-0.44	-0.41	-0.45	-0.36	-0.27	-0.06	-0.42	0.09
Family income below poverty level	-0.46	-0.36	-0.51	-0.39	-0.29	0.00	-0.27	0.13
Family income less than 200 percent of poverty level	-0.39	-0.33	-0.44	-0.33	-0.26	-0.02	-0.58	0.19
Wages less than $8.00 per hour	-0.42	-0.42	-0.41	-0.44	-0.27	0.01	-0.24	-0.47
Period	1993 to 1995	1999 to 2001	1993 to 1995	1999 to 2001	1993 to 1995	1999 to 2001	1993 to 1995	1999 to 2001
High school dropouts	-0.28	-0.32	-0.31	-0.22	-0.37	-0.05	-0.38	-0.06
High school dropouts and graduates	-0.44	-0.32	-0.44	-0.38	-0.36	-0.15	-0.28	-0.03
Family income below poverty level	-0.44	-0.34	-0.25	-0.18	-0.52	-0.20	-0.33	-0.07
Family income less than 200 percent of poverty level	-0.32	-0.32	-0.42	-0.35	-0.41	-0.12	-0.33	0.04
Wages less than $8.00 per hour	-0.43	-0.48	-0.44	-0.43	-0.33	-0.27	-0.31	0.14

Source: Authors' compilation.

what more likely to work for better firms; and those who made complete escapes out of low earnings worked for considerably better firms. In fact, this appears to be just as true for the subsamples of low earners whom we consider here—including the less-educated, those in lower-income families, and those earning low wages—as it is for the overall sample. Increases in average firm fixed effects over time are also more pronounced among those who made relatively more complete transitions out of low earnings within each of these subsamples.

Overall, the data presented here on subsamples of low earners matched to the CPS confirm our primary results from this chapter. On the one hand, it seems as though many in our samples of low earners were not from low-income families or did not have very low educational attainment, though their hourly wages were low and most were in families below 200 percent of the poverty line. When we restrict our attention to those who did have low education and low family income, we find somewhat lower but still substantial rates of transition out of low earnings, as well as very important correlations between such transitions and firm characteristics. In other words, while substantial numbers in our original samples of low earners may not have had low educational attainment or low family incomes, the frequencies and correlates of transitions out of low earnings that we observed earlier are fairly consistent with what we find here for those low earners who really are disadvantaged.

We thus conclude that the results presented in this chapter are quite informative with respect to earnings advancement issues for low earners with poor skills and/or low family incomes.

Chapter Five | Moving Up or On: The Role of Job Mobility in Raising Earnings

THE EVIDENCE IN the previous chapter confirms that the characteristics of the firms for which they work, and especially the wage premia paid by those firms, have important effects on the likelihood that low earners will advance in the labor market. The evidence in chapter 4 also shows that the characteristics of the employers for whom initial low earners worked improved over time, thereby contributing to their improved earnings.

These findings raise broader questions about whether low earners succeed more frequently in the labor market through job *retention* or job *mobility*. Job retention is staying in the same initial job and with the same initial employer, even if that employer generally pays low wages. The worker's wages may improve over time because he or she is accumulating experience and seniority on the job and acquiring on-the-job training. Job mobility is moving across jobs—perhaps from a lower-wage to a higher-wage employer—and reaping the benefits in terms of higher earnings levels after the job change.[1]

Of course, whether or not low earners are able to gain access to higher-wage employers affects their ability to improve their status through job mobility. And even if they can do so, there are often costs involved—perhaps in the form of earnings forgone during a period of non-employment between jobs or lost wage increases that they would have earned with longer experience and more seniority at the initial firm.[2]

On the other hand, the cost of lost wage increases will not be great if the returns to seniority on the initial job are not very high in the first place—that is, if that job is fairly "dead-end" and offers few opportunities for advancement. Indeed, rates of turnover out of low-wage jobs may be high precisely because the returns to staying in those jobs are fairly low. As the literature we reviewed in chapter 1 suggests, low earners experience on-the-job wage growth, but the magnitudes are often fairly modest; the evidence that job mobility is productive for these workers is mixed as well.[3]

Furthermore, the standard theory of "human capital" in labor economics suggests a trade-off between initial wage levels and subsequent wage growth, implying that low levels of earnings initially might be necessary to achieve higher earnings growth over time. But it is much less clear that this is true *across* rather than *within* jobs. In other words, while an individual might need to forgo some of his or her initial earnings within any job in order to receive on-the-job training from the employer, it is not clear that working in low-wage jobs or firms relative to higher-wage ones offers greater potential for wage growth over time; indeed, high-wage firms might well provide a very different set of human resource policies, including more training for their workers.[4] Thus, it is possible that earnings growth for low earners in low-paying firms requires an initial period of mobility to a better job, perhaps followed by a period of job stability to accumulate job tenure and gain on-the-job training (formal or informal) once such a job is attained.

Of course, no such evidence would imply that high turnover per se is a good strategy for low earners. Indeed, it is not job mobility alone that is likely to be successful, but rather *job mobility in the presence of opportunities for work at higher-wage firms and jobs.*[5] But the extent to which these opportunities exist and the extent to which they drive the job mobility or earnings growth of initial low earners have not been well established to date.

In this chapter, we provide evidence on these issues. Our first goal is to present data on the extent of job mobility among low earners and on the relationship between that mobility and observed transitions out of low earnings for them. We consider mobility across jobs in the six years subsequent to our initial observations on low earnings, and we look at different patterns of job moving and staying during that time. Once we establish which patterns are associated with higher earnings transitions and growth, we then ask whether (and to what extent) it is the characteristics of the workers or the jobs they attain that are associated with these patterns.

Furthermore, we look at whether some attributes of the work experience during the initial period of low earnings—such as accumulating tenure with an earlier employer, working with a temp agency, or working earlier at a high-wage firm—improve the quality of the subsequent job attained and therefore of the future earnings of these workers. The issue of early work experience speaks to whether "work-first" strategies for welfare recipients and other low earners might generate improved employment outcomes over time, and the issue of working with temp agencies raises the broader question of whether these and other "labor market intermediaries" can improve the quality of the jobs and firms to which low earners have access over time.

As in the earlier chapter, we begin with descriptive data that establish the basic relationships between job mobility, transitions out of low earnings, and both person and job characteristics of low earners. Once we establish these facts, we move to multiple regression analysis of the determinants of both earnings and turnover behavior to infer the relative magnitudes of various person and firm effects in generating the outcomes we observe. At least initially, we limit ourselves (as before) to analysis of retention with or mobility across "primary employers" over three-year periods. When we turn to the regression analysis, however, we once again consider each person-quarter as an observation and consider all jobs held by any worker in the relevant time period.

TURNOVER AND EARNINGS TRANSITIONS AMONG LOW EARNERS

We begin by looking at the extent to which low earners moved across jobs in the six years subsequent to the base period (1993 to 1995), during which time we designate them as low earners. Figure 5.1 presents the percentages of these low earners who stayed with the same primary employer in the period 1996 to 1998 versus those who moved to another job. We also provide the same percentages for the period 1999 to 2001, both overall and conditional on whether the individuals changed employers during the 1996 to 1998 period.

The data in figure 5.1 imply that about half of all low earners in the initial period stayed with the same primary employer in the subsequent three years while about half changed to a different one. Of course, these rates of mobility across primary employers no doubt understate the true degree of turnover and job mobility for this population.[6] Furthermore, the data show that nearly 40 percent of these workers changed their primary employer another time during the 1999 to 2001 period. Among those who changed employers during the intermediary period, rates of subsequent job change are much higher (above 60 percent) than among those who initially stayed (about 30 percent). Thus, there seem to be individuals who habitually changed jobs or remained with their employer, while others combined some degree of job-changing and job-staying over the six-year period.

To what extent is observed job-changing related to transitions out of low earnings and to earnings growth over that time period? Tables 5.1 and 5.2 present data on job mobility and transitions out of low earnings; the latter include both partial and complete transitions, as defined earlier.

Figure 5.1   Rates of Job Mobility in 1993 to 1995 Versus 1996 to
              1998 and in 1996 to 1998 Versus 1999 to 2001:
              Workers with Low Earnings in 1993 to 1995

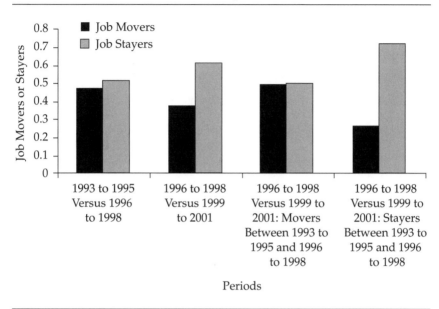

Source: Authors' compilation.
Note: "Job mobility" is defined as a change in primary employer between periods.

Also as before, we limit the samples here to those who were persistently
low earners during the 1993 to 1995 base period.

   There are, in fact, two ways of presenting that relationship. One involves presenting the rate of transitions out of low earnings, conditional
on whether individuals have changed their primary employer; the other
involves the extent to which individuals change employers, conditional
on whether they have transitioned out of low earnings. Essentially, the
former presents the success rate associated with each type of behavior,
while the latter provides the extent to which one or another behavior accounts for any observed success.[7] We provide the former data in table 5.1
and the latter in table 5.2.

   Furthermore, we first present the job mobility patterns as simple binary
outcomes—either primary job-moving or job-staying—across successive
three-year periods. However, over the two three-year periods subsequent
to the base period, we also identify four possible combinations of job
mobility outcomes: "move-move," "move-stay," "stay-move," and "stay-

Table 5.1   Distribution of Initial Low Earners Across Transition
             Categories, by Job Mobility

	Earnings Status in 1996 to 1998			
	Still Low	Partial Escape	Full Escape	All
Job mobility in 1993 to 1995 versus 1996 to 1998				
All	0.43	0.48	0.08	1.00
Move	0.30	0.57	0.13	1.00
Stay	0.56	0.41	0.04	1.00
	Earnings Status in 1999 to 2001			
	Still Low	Partial Escape	Full Escape	All
Job mobility in 1996 to 1998 versus 1999 to 2001				
All	0.57	0.39	0.04	1.00
Move	0.40	0.51	0.08	1.00
Stay	0.65	0.33	0.02	1.00
	Earnings Status in 1999 to 2001			
	Still Low	Partial Escape	Full Escape	All
Job mobility in 1993 to 1995 versus 1996 to 1998 and in 1996 to 1998 versus 1999 to 2001				
All	0.29	0.44	0.28	1.00
Move-move	0.19	0.49	0.31	1.00
Move-stay	0.19	0.39	0.42	1.00
Stay-move	0.24	0.49	0.27	1.00
Stay-stay	0.42	0.40	0.17	1.00

Source: Authors' compilation.
Note: Earnings status in the middle panel is defined only for those who were still low earners in 1996 to 1998.

stay," indicating the observed combination of mobility outcomes in the first-second of these two subsequent periods.

The data clearly indicate that *job-movers have higher rates of transitions out of low earnings than do job-stayers.* For instance, the rates of complete escape out of low earnings are 13 percent for movers and 4 percent for stayers in the 1996 to 1998 period, respectively, and the rates of partial or com-

Table 5.2   Distribution of Initial Low Earners Across Job Mobility
Categories, by Escape Status

	Earnings Status in 1996 to 1998			
	Still Low	Partial Escape	Full Escape	All
Job mobility in 1993 to 1995 versus 1996 to 1998				
Move	0.33	0.56	0.76	0.47
Stay	0.67	0.44	0.24	0.53
All	1.00	1.00	1.00	1.00
	Earnings Status in 1999 to 2001			
	Still Low	Partial Escape	Full Escape	All
Job mobility in 1996 to 1998 versus 1999 to 2001				
Move	0.24	0.44	0.66	0.34
Stay	0.76	0.56	0.34	0.66
All	1.00	1.00	1.00	1.00
	Earnings Status in 1999 to 2001			
	Still Low	Partial Escape	Full Escape	All
Job mobility in 1993 to 1995 versus 1996 to 1998 and in 1996 to 1998 versus 1999 to 2001				
Move-move	0.16	0.27	0.27	0.24
Move-stay	0.16	0.22	0.36	0.24
Stay-move	0.12	0.16	0.14	0.14
Stay-stay	0.56	0.36	0.24	0.38
All	1.00	1.00	1.00	1.00

Source: Authors' compilation.
Note: Earnings status in the middle panel is defined only for those who were still low earners in 1996 to 1998.

plete escape are about 70 percent and 45 percent, respectively. Among those who remained low earners during that period, the comparable rates of complete escape in the 1999 to 2001 period are 8 percent for movers and 2 percent for stayers, respectively, while the rates of partial or complete escape are about 60 percent and 35 percent, respectively.

Furthermore, when combining job mobility outcomes across both subsequent periods, we find that *the highest rates of both partial and complete escape out of low earnings are observed for those who changed jobs initially (in 1996 to 1998) and then stayed with their new employer (in 1999 to 2001)*—in other words, for those who "move-stay.[8] Specifically, over 40 percent of all initial low earners who moved out of a job and then stayed in the next one escaped low earnings completely, and another nearly 40 percent did so partially. Those who moved in the first period and then moved again also did relatively well, with about 30 percent escaping low earnings completely and about 50 percent escaping partially. Transitions out of low earnings for those who stayed with the same employer initially and then moved in the subsequent period are somewhat lower, at 27 percent and 49 percent, respectively, for complete and partial escapes, and those who perpetually stayed with the same primary employer for whom they worked in the base period have the lowest rates of transition (17 percent and 40 percent, respectively).

Thus, the results indicate that, while changing employers is generally a relatively more successful strategy than staying with the same one, *a combination of earlier job mobility and subsequent job retention may work best for low earners.* Such a combination might allow for a move to a better employer with a higher wage premium, as well as the accumulation of seniority and on-the-job training at the better firm and wage returns to that seniority over time. Perpetual movement across employers might impede the accumulation of seniority and training and often generates periods of non-employment and lost earnings between jobs, but such mobility still seems to generate higher earnings than does delayed movement across employers or no movement at all.[9]

Of course, these findings remain suggestive at this point and must await a more careful multivariate analysis of the characteristics of people who move or stay as well as of the jobs to which they attach in each case. And even if we confirm the findings about returns to job-moving and job-staying, decisions to move or stay may simply reflect the appropriate choices for the individuals who are making them rather than represent a prescription for behavior that can be generalized more broadly to low earners.[10]

Nonetheless, the observed patterns of earnings transitions and job mobility over the longer term are striking.

Given the higher rates of earnings transitions associated with job-moving in general and with early moving and subsequent job retention in particular, to what extent does each mobility pattern account for observed transitions out of low earnings? Table 5.2 implies that *mobility across jobs accounts for most of the observed transitions out of low earnings.* For instance, job-movers account for over three-fourths of complete escapes out of low earnings in the 1996 to 1998 period and for well over half of partial escapes. For those who remained low earners in that period, job-movers account for about two-thirds of complete escapes but under half of partial escapes in the 1999 to 2001 period.

And combining patterns of mobility across the two periods, we find that those who moved initially and then retained their new jobs account for over one-third of all complete transitions out of low earnings and that those who moved initially (and either stayed or changed jobs again in the subsequent period) account for nearly two-thirds of all full escapes over the six-year period.

Overall, the results suggest that it is certainly not impossible to stay with the same employer over time and still escape low earnings, especially considering the possibility of a partial, as opposed to a complete, transition. In fact, those who stayed with the same primary employer over all six years subsequent to the base period account for nearly one-fourth of all complete transitions and about one-third of partial ones. At the same time, the data suggest that the odds of escaping low earnings are higher for those who change jobs, especially relatively earlier on, and that such changes account for the lion's share of successful transitions out of low earnings over time.

What rates of earnings growth and employment are achieved by those who change jobs as opposed to those who do not? Do those who change jobs have lower observed rates of employment and even more total job changes than are implied by the data on primary employers? Are their rates of earnings growth on the same job limited because of their movement across employers? Some further evidence on these issues appears in table 5.3, where we present data on mean earnings growth, quarters of employment, number of employers, and tenure over the six-year period subsequent to the base period for initial low earners according to their pattern of job mobility over that time period.

The results largely confirm what we observed from the data on transitions in table 5.1—namely, that earnings growth is generally higher for job-movers than for job-stayers, and especially for those who move early but then subsequently stay with the same primary employer. The fact that mean earnings rise more quickly among job-movers than job-stayers implies that the higher transitions out of low earnings that we observed in tables 5.1 and 5.2 do not simply reflect a higher variance in earnings changes among job-changers, such that negative transitions among nonlow earners may simply offset positive transitions among low earners.

But we also find some evidence of the costs entailed when individuals change jobs. For one thing, we find fewer quarters of employment among the job-changers, and especially among the repeat changers. We also note

Table 5.3   Mean Earnings and Employment, by Job Mobility
Categories

| | Job Mobility 1993 to 1995 Versus 1996 to 1998 and 1996 to 1998 Versus 1999 to 2001 | | | |
	Move-Move	Move-Stay	Stay-Move	Stay-Stay
Annual earnings				
1993 to 1995	$7,259	$7,419	$7,714	$7,720
1996 to 1998	12,972	14,101	10,722	10,520
1999 to 2001	17,562	18,679	15,896	13,094
Quarterly earnings				
1993 to 1995	2,110	2,131	2,127	2,107
1996 to 1998	3,471	3,703	2,832	2,765
1999 to 2001	4,645	4,838	4,171	3,445
Quarterly tenure				
1993 to 1995	7.73	9.08	11.20	12.73
1996 to 1998	7.75	9.78	20.39	24.12
1999 to 2001	9.73	20.53	10.62	35.19
Quarters worked				
1993 to 1995	10.44	10.58	10.99	11.16
1996 to 1998	11.16	11.41	11.36	11.52
1999 to 2001	11.24	11.52	11.36	11.44
Change in quarters worked, 1993 to 1995 to 1999 to 2001	0.81	0.94	0.38	0.28
Number of employers				
1993 to 1995	3.84	2.80	1.97	1.43
1996 to 1998	3.73	2.18	2.14	1.17
1999 to 2001	2.81	1.45	2.08	1.23

Source: Authors' compilation.

that the number of employers held by the repeat job-changers is quite high
and that accumulation of tenure is lower than among any other group.
Earnings growth thus appears lower for the repeat job-changers than for
those who change jobs early and then retain those jobs, as we might expect.

JOB-CHANGERS VERSUS JOB-STAYERS: CHARACTERISTICS OF WORKERS AND FIRMS

Although the preceding data suggest that there are strong returns to
changing jobs in some circumstances and to keeping them in others, it is

Table 5.4   Job Mobility, by Personal Characteristics

	Job Mobility 1993 to 1995 Versus 1996 to 1998 and 1996 to 1998 Versus 1999 to 2001				
	Move-Move	Move-Stay	Stay-Move	Stay-Stay	All
All workers	0.24	0.24	0.14	0.38	1.00
By race-ethnicity and gender					
White females	0.18	0.23	0.14	0.45	1.00
Black females	0.30	0.25	0.15	0.31	1.00
Asian females	0.23	0.24	0.15	0.38	1.00
Hispanic females	0.20	0.24	0.16	0.41	1.00
White males	0.31	0.24	0.14	0.31	1.00
Black males	0.41	0.27	0.11	0.21	1.00
Asian males	0.28	0.28	0.14	0.29	1.00
Hispanic males	0.30	0.26	0.16	0.28	1.00
By place of birth					
Foreign-born	0.22	0.25	0.16	0.38	1.00
U.S.-born	0.24	0.24	0.14	0.38	1.00
By age					
25 to 34	0.34	0.27	0.15	0.25	1.00
35 to 44	0.20	0.23	0.15	0.42	1.00
45 to 54	0.14	0.20	0.13	0.53	1.00
By person fixed effect (quartile)					
First	0.18	0.21	0.14	0.46	1.00
Second	0.31	0.27	0.15	0.27	1.00
Third	0.36	0.29	0.14	0.21	1.00
Fourth	0.33	0.28	0.11	0.27	1.00

Source: Authors' compilation.

also possible that these results are driven by the personal characteristics of those who choose to change (or stay in) jobs or by the characteristics of the jobs that they move into (relative to those they leave behind). Our regression analysis presented later in the chapter attempts to disentangle these factors; here we present some summary data on the personal characteristics of job-changers and job-stayers as well as on the jobs they hold at different points in time.

Table 5.4 presents the percentages of initially low-earning workers who moved from and/or stayed at their jobs in the two subsequent periods, separately for race-ethnicity and gender, place of birth, and age. The data show, for instance, that low-earning men are more likely to change jobs than women and that younger (prime-age) workers change jobs more frequently than older ones. These facts certainly indicate that many personal circumstances and characteristics—such as family commitments or the fixed costs of changing residences—affect job turnover and job retention patterns independently of labor market circumstances. These findings are also consistent with the earlier ones (in chapter 4) showing higher rates of transition out of low earnings for men and younger workers, and they suggest that these personal characteristics of job-changers are partly responsible for their greater success.

On the other hand, we also find that blacks are more likely than whites to change jobs, even though they tend to escape low earnings less frequently than whites. This confirms that not all job mobility is productive and suggests that a greater proportion of the turnover experienced by blacks is attributable to poor job performance, poor job characteristics, or racial differences in the workplace.[11] Differences in job mobility rates between whites, Asians, and Hispanics, or between those born in the United States and those born elsewhere, are quite small. And differences in demographics between perpetual movers and those who move initially and then stay on their new jobs are small in almost all cases. Thus, the personal characteristics of workers do not seem to account for all of the differences in success rates observed across workers with different job mobility patterns.

How do the characteristics of firms vary across patterns of job mobility for workers? Tables 5.5 and 5.6 present the characteristics of the primary firms for which initial low earners worked in the base period and in subsequent periods, separately by their mobility patterns. We present the industries for which they worked in table 5.5; firm sizes, turnover rates, and firm wage premia are provided in table 5.6. These data enable us to compare the kinds of firms these workers were leaving behind or staying with in the two earlier periods, as well as the kinds of firms they were attached to in the final period. The data can thus shed light on how firm characteristics help to determine mobility across jobs and also how these characteristics are changed by the resulting mobility.

The results on industries show that those who moved in each period tend to be more concentrated in retail trade, while those who stayed tend to be heavily concentrated in services. Even in the middle period, those who moved and those who stayed (either for the first or the second time) are concentrated in these sectors, respectively. The fact that young workers are more likely to be in retail trade and that women are relatively more concentrated in the services is consistent with these results. By the final period the movers have become relatively more concentrated than the

Table 5.5   Distribution of Workers Across Industries, by Mobility Status

| | Job Mobility 1993 to 1995 Versus 1996 to 1998 and 1996 to 1998 Versus 1999 to 2001 | | | |
	Move-Move	Move-Stay	Stay-Move	Stay-Stay
By industry in 1993 to 1995				
Construction	0.04	0.03	0.03	0.03
Manufacturing	0.12	0.10	0.11	0.08
Transportation and utilities	0.03	0.03	0.02	0.02
Wholesale trade	0.03	0.03	0.03	0.03
Retail trade	0.34	0.35	0.36	0.24
Finance, insurance, and real estate	0.03	0.03	0.03	0.03
Services	0.40	0.41	0.41	0.55
Public administration	0.01	0.01	0.01	0.02
All	1.00	1.00	1.00	1.00
By industry in 1996 to 1998				
Construction	0.04	0.04	0.03	0.03
Manufacturing	0.13	0.14	0.11	0.09
Transportation and utilities	0.04	0.04	0.02	0.02
Wholesale trade	0.05	0.05	0.03	0.03
Retail trade	0.26	0.26	0.36	0.23
Finance, insurance, and real estate	0.05	0.04	0.03	0.03
Services	0.42	0.41	0.40	0.55
Public administration	0.01	0.03	0.01	0.02
All	1.00	1.00	1.00	1.00
By industry in 1999 to 2001				
Construction	0.05	0.04	0.03	0.03
Manufacturing	0.14	0.14	0.12	0.09
Transportation and utilities	0.04	0.04	0.03	0.02
Wholesale trade	0.05	0.05	0.05	0.03
Retail trade	0.22	0.26	0.27	0.24
Finance, insurance, and real estate	0.06	0.04	0.05	0.03
Services	0.42	0.41	0.43	0.54
Public administration	0.02	0.03	0.03	0.02
All	1.00	1.00	1.00	1.00

Source: Authors' compilation.

Table 5.6   Distribution of Workers Across Firm Size, Annual Worker
Turnover, and Firm Fixed Effect Categories, by Job Mobility Status

	Move-Move		Move-Stay		Stay-Move		Stay-Stay	
	Mean	Median	Mean	Median	Mean	Median	Mean	Median
Firm size								
1993 to 1995	2,187	118	2,768	107	2,511	97	4,883	207
1996 to 1998	2,170	162	3,975	210	2,628	100	5,207	228
1999 to 2001	3,232	245	4,472	233	3,444	249	5,566	244
Annual worker turnover								
1993 to 1995	0.62	0.61	0.59	0.57	0.54	0.52	0.43	0.38
1996 to 1998	0.60	0.59	0.50	0.48	0.46	0.44	0.35	0.31
1999 to 2001	0.53	0.50	0.41	0.39	0.50	0.48	0.36	0.32
Firm fixed effect								
1993 to 1995	−0.29	−0.27	−0.31	−0.29	−0.34	−0.31	−0.30	−0.24
1996 to 1998	−0.16	−0.14	−0.13	−0.11	−0.34	−0.31	−0.30	−0.24
1999 to 2001	−0.07	−0.05	−0.13	−0.11	−0.15	−0.12	−0.30	−0.24

Source: Authors' compilation.

stayers in high-wage sectors such as construction, manufacturing, and transportation.

As for differences in mobility patterns by establishment size and turnover rate, in table 5.6 we find that initial low earners were more likely to stay in larger firms and to move out of smaller ones in the first two periods, as well as more likely to stay in low-turnover firms and to move out of high-turnover ones.[12] By the final period, movers were more concentrated in larger and low-turnover establishments than they were initially.

And the data show that the propensity of workers to move seems moderately related to their firm's wage premia in the earlier periods. In particular, there is relatively little relationship between moving-staying and the firm wage premium in the initial period. But repeat movers had somewhat lower firm wage premia in their second jobs than those who initially moved but then stayed in their newer jobs, and those who initially stayed and then moved certainly had lower wage premia in the second period than did persistent stayers. Furthermore, moving seems generally associated with improving firm wage premia in subsequent periods—and those who moved repeatedly ended up with the best firms of all (in terms of wage premia).

Thus, mobility patterns are consistent with the notion of job-changers moving toward higher-wage firms and sectors of the economy. At the same time, job mobility is not very strongly or consistently related to initial firm wage premia. No doubt, other characteristics of the jobs them-selves—such as the benefits they provided, the shift schedules and hours, and the location of the firm—contributed to the mobility and retention de-cisions of these workers as well. The final results also show that the group with the highest earnings—those who moved initially and then stayed in their new job—improved their wage premia relative to those of stayers but that in the end they did not have the highest wage premia of all groups. Thus, the characteristics of firms help account for who left earlier jobs and where they went, but they do not seem to fully account for the mobility patterns observed or the differences in transitions out of low earnings that we find across groups with different job mobility patterns.

BASE PERIOD JOBS AMONG MOVERS: THE ROLE OF EARLY TENURE AND TEMP AGENCIES

These data suggest that job-changing, especially when it results in em-ployment at a higher-wage firm, is an important mechanism by which ini-tial low earners transition out of this status. On the other hand, it is still possible that certain characteristics and experiences of these early jobs contribute to the transitions that low earners make to other jobs—not right away, but eventually.

For example, proponents of "work-first" strategies for welfare recipi-ents and others with low work experience suggest that some early work experience, even in a low-wage job, is important for later wage growth. While upward mobility is limited in many early jobs, attaining at least some amount of steady work experience (or tenure) with particular em-ployers may signal general skill acquisition and job-readiness to other po-tential employers.[13] On the other hand, by working in a higher-wage job, an individual may acquire training or skills that are more transferable to other higher-wage jobs in the same or similar sectors of the economy.

Similarly, the role of employment at temp agencies for low earners has been controversial (see, for instance, Autor and Houseman 2002b). While they are working for temp agencies, less-educated workers earn lower wages and benefits than do comparable workers in other agencies. On the other hand, it is at least possible that these workers gain greater early work experience, as well as links to better employers, than they would be able to achieve on their own. Temp agencies may also represent the po-tential inherent in a broader range of labor market "intermediaries" to im-prove the quality of jobs to which low-skill workers have access, thus per-haps leading to better earnings in the future, if not right away.

We test these hypotheses explicitly in the multiple regression analysis

Table 5.7   Tenure and Temp Agency Employment in the Base Period
            Among Low Earners Who Changed Jobs, by Earnings
            Status in Later Periods

	Tenure		Fraction of All Workers Employed in Temp Agencies
	Mean	Median	
Earnings in 1997 to 1999			
Still low	8.96	9	0.05
Partial escape	8.27	8	0.06
Full escape	7.67	7	0.07
Earnings in 1999 to 2001			
Still low	9.16	9	0.05
Partial escape	8.23	8	0.06
Full escape	8.23	8	0.06

Source: Authors' compilation.

presented later in the chapter, but in the meantime we provide some summary evidence on these issues. In table 5.7, we present data for job-changers only on transition rates out of low earnings by the characteristics of early work experience—including tenure and the wage premia of the earlier job—as well as by whether the individual worked for a temp agency initially.

The results show that *initial low earners are less likely to remain as low earners in the subsequent period if they worked at temp agencies earlier.* This is true both in the base period (1993 to 1995) and also in the first period subsequent to the base period (1996 to 1998). The data suggest that temps specifically—and perhaps labor market intermediaries more broadly—can play a positive role in improving the success of low earners over time. Whether they do so by improving access to better jobs or by simply providing workers with some early work experience is explored later. The relationship between early job tenure and subsequent success is not positive in these data, though the regression results presented in this chapter do suggest a more positive relationship.

These data thus suggest that, even while workers are low earners, having certain kinds of work experience improves the chances for subsequent success. On the other hand, having *any* kind of early work experience has some positive effect but does not uniformly improve subsequent outcomes. We explore these factors more fully in our regression analysis.

RESULTS OF MULTIPLE REGRESSION ANALYSIS: DETERMINANTS OF QUARTERLY EARNINGS

The next few tables present results from multiple regression analysis of quarterly earnings. The dependent variable is the ln(quarterly earnings) in all cases, while the sample is limited to individuals who were persistent low earners in the base period (1993 to 1995). The observations used here are all person-quarters of employment in the period 1999 to 2001; using only this final period enables us to avoid endogeneity problems with some of our independent variables, such as the person fixed effects or the variables on mobility patterns across the two subsequent periods (move-move, move-stay, and so on).[14]

The goal of these regressions is to analyze the effects of patterns of job-moving on earnings over time. In particular, we are interested in trying to account for the summary results presented earlier: job-movers had higher earnings transitions and growth than job-stayers, but earlier movers who then stayed on their subsequent job had the highest transition rates and earnings growth of all. To what extent do the characteristics of the workers themselves account for these patterns, and to what extent are these patterns attributable to the characteristics of their jobs? What role is played by the accumulation of job tenure? Job tenure is lost among those who move but may be accumulated by those who stay on their new job. Are there different returns to tenure according to the wage premium of the firm and/or different degrees of job mobility? If so, what accounts for these differences?

To answer these questions, we have run these regressions separately for each of the four groups defined by mobility pattern (move-move, move-stay, and so on).[15] Independent variables in each equation include some characteristics of the workers themselves, such as the fixed person effect and potential experience; the characteristic of the job, as measured by the fixed firm effect; worker tenure, with both a linear and a quadratic term; and interactions between the firm effect and the tenure variables. As usual, positive linear but negative quadratic terms should capture a gradually declining effect of increasing tenure on earnings over time.[16] The interactions are designed to test whether the returns to tenure are higher or lower at high-wage firms than at lower-wage ones. We also include a dummy variable for whether each quarter was a "full" quarter to capture the possible costs of job mobility in terms of lost earnings.

The regression coefficients themselves appear in table 5.8. The results are generally as expected. Personal characteristics, such as the person

Table 5.8   Regressions of Log Quarterly Earnings, by Mobility Group

	Stay-Stay	Stay-Move	Move-Stay	Move-Move
Person fixed effect	0.661	0.306	0.567	0.410
	(153.86)**	(41.11)**	(108.94)**	(62.73)**
Experience	0.014	0.005	0.009	0.005
	(35.44)**	(7.43)**	(22.10)**	(10.75)**
Squared experience	−0.035	−0.014	−0.021	−0.011
	(19.91)**	(4.53)**	(10.17)**	(4.21)**
Firm fixed effect	0.561	0.536	0.868	0.699
	(23.19)**	(29.84)**	(36.46)**	(50.37)**
Tenure	0.017	0.044	0.039	0.047
	(16.49)**	(27.28)**	(26.67)**	(34.43)**
Squared tenure	−0.113	−1.548	−0.899	−1.632
	(4.89)**	(26.83)**	(18.13)**	(26.19)**
Tenure × firm fixed effect	0.008	0.027	0.007	0.022
	(4.08)**	(7.80)**	(2.04)*	(7.32)**
Squared tenure × firm fixed effect	−0.071	−0.926	−0.213	−0.839
	−1.57	(8.09)**	−1.940	(7.13)**
Full quarter employed	0.164	0.347	0.254	0.448
	(29.40)**	(46.04)**	(41.02)**	(78.76)**
Constant	7.114	7.570	7.450	7.513
	(318.82)**	(239.96)**	(339.03)**	(320.88)**
Observations	119,016	46,146	77,481	75,872
R-squared	0.20	0.21	0.31	0.28

Source: Authors' compilation.
Notes: All specifications include a full set of state dummies (not reported). Absolute values of t statistics are in parentheses.
*significant at 5 percent; **significant at 1 percent

fixed effect, have strong positive effects on earnings. The effects of experience and also tenure are positive in all cases, but with negative quadratic terms that confirm their diminishing effects over time. The firm fixed effect has a strong and positive effect on wages; its interaction with tenure also has positive effects on earnings (while the interactions with the quadratic term are negative) for each mobility group as well.

These positive interactions confirm that *returns to tenure for each group are higher in higher-wage firms.* This implies that there is no trade-off across

Figure 5.2   Wage-Tenure Profiles, by Mobility Group

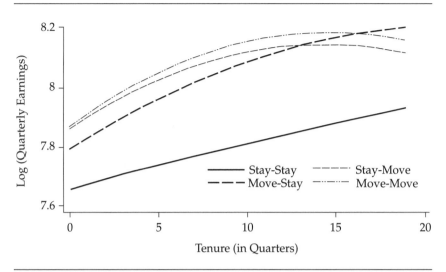

Source: Authors' compilation.
Note: Mean tenure for the stay-stay group is 29.1 quarters; 8.3 for stay-movers; 14.9 for move-stayers; and 6.4 for move-movers.

firms between initial wage levels and wage growth over time, but rather that the firms that pay higher wages also provide the most upward mobility through on-the-job training, promotion ladders, and other human resource policies.

In general, returns to tenure and firm effects are larger for job-movers than for job-stayers, perhaps indicating that the greater returns to these characteristics motivated the decisions of the movers to change their jobs in the first place. In contrast, personal characteristics—like experience—have their strongest effects for those staying in their original jobs.[17] The coefficients on the full-quarter variable also suggest that some substantial costs per quarter are associated with mobility and that these costs are especially large for recent job movers (35 to 45 percent) and could quickly cumulate for those who change jobs frequently.

In figure 5.2, we plot the returns to estimated returns to tenure for each of the four groups.[18] Also, to get a better sense of how returns to tenure vary across mobility patterns as well as with the firm wage premium, we have plotted the returns to tenure across quarters of work with the firm for each of the four mobility groups, and with separate profiles within each group for those at the twenty-fifty, fiftieth, and seventy-fifth percentiles in terms of firm fixed effect. These appear in figure 5.3. Since average tenure

Figure 5.3 Wage-Tenure Profiles, by Mobility Group and Firm Fixed Effect

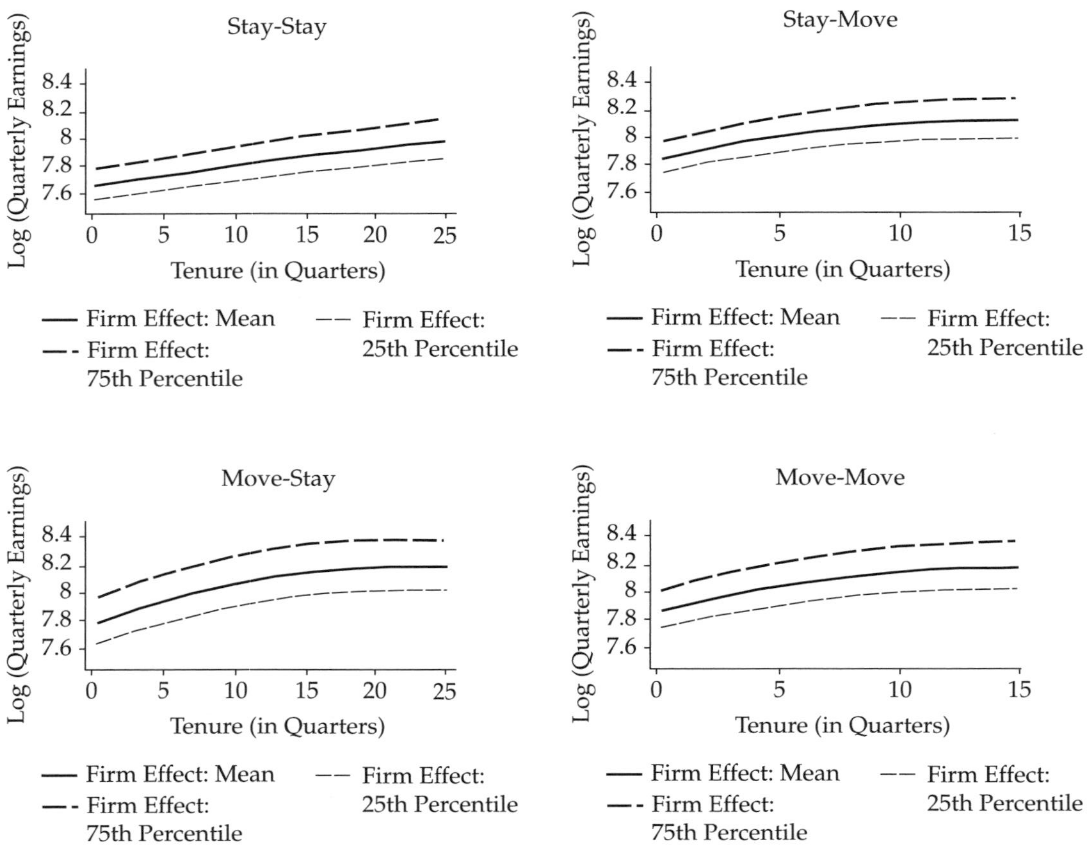

Stay-Stay
Log (Quarterly Earnings)
8.4
8.2
8
7.8
7.6
0
5
10
15
20
25
Tenure (in Quarters)
Firm Effect: Mean
Firm Effect: 75th Percentile
Firm Effect: 25th Percentile
Stay-Move
Log (Quarterly Earnings)
Tenure (in Quarters)
Firm Effect: Mean
Firm Effect: 75th Percentile
Firm Effect: 25th Percentile
Move-Stay
Log (Quarterly Earnings)
Tenure (in Quarters)
Firm Effect: Mean
Firm Effect: 75th Percentile
Firm Effect: 25th Percentile
Move-Move
Log (Quarterly Earnings)
Tenure (in Quarters)
Firm Effect: Mean
Firm Effect: 75th Percentile
Firm Effect: 25th Percentile

Source: Authors' compilation.

is much shorter among those who moved recently than among those who did not, we plot returns to about twenty-five quarters among recent job-stayers and ten to fifteen quarters for recent job-changers.

The plots present some important results. It is clear that the levels of earnings are generally lower for those who stayed in their original job over the entire six-year period, relative to the different groups of job-changers. Not only did job-changers improve their initial earnings levels considerably compared to the initial levels earned by job-stayers, but they also enjoyed higher rates of earnings growth over time—at least for the first three years or so on their new jobs.

But the returns to tenure were sufficiently high, even for the perpetual job-stayers, that the mean level of tenure accumulated by these individuals tended to mitigate their earnings shortfall relative to the job-movers and perhaps reinforced their decisions to stay on these jobs. The view that these low-wage jobs are all "dead-end" in nature is not supported by these data, as Tricia Gladden and Christopher Taber (2000) have argued.

Comparing the different groups of job-movers to one another, we find that those who moved originally and then stayed in their new jobs began these new jobs with somewhat lower wages than the more recent movers earned, but then the higher tenure they accumulated over time raised their earnings relative to the recent movers. The tendency of their returns to tenure to fade out more slowly (with returns that are more linear and less quadratic than those of the other groups) tends to reinforce this effect.

In the plots in figure 5.3, we also find some modest "fanning out" of the earnings graphs with tenure, especially among the recent movers. This implies higher returns to tenure among those in the seventy-fifth percentiles of firm fixed effects than among those with lower firm effects. Even where little fanning out is observed, earnings increased more rapidly among the higher earners in absolute terms.[19]

Thus, the figures confirm that, when low earners move to new jobs, they often find better opportunities for higher earnings levels and growth over time, but that some significant cost is attached to the loss of job tenure for repeat or later job changes.

To what extent are the differences in average earnings observed across the four mobility groups in the final period—with movers of all kinds generally having higher earnings than job-stayers—accounted for by differences in job tenure and firm characteristics across these groups? How much do these earnings differences depend on differences across groups in the *levels* of these characteristics, as opposed to differences in the labor market *returns* to these factors?

To answer these questions, we have decomposed the overall earnings differences across these four groups according to the technique attributed to Alan Blinder (1973) and Ronald Oaxaca (1973). In this technique, the mean values of each variable for one group are combined with the coefficients from estimated regressions of another group to generate "predicted earnings." Comparisons between predicted and actual earnings across various pairs of groups then indicate the extent to which differences across groups in characteristics or returns to those characteristics account for the overall observed earnings differences across groups. Furthermore, the contribution of differences in each group characteristic and its coefficient to overall observed differences can also be ascertained by considering the individual components of the predicted earnings measures.[20]

Results of these decompositions, using the regression coefficients from table 5.8 and differences in means across the groups, appear for tenure and the firm fixed effects (and their interactions) as well as the full quarter dummies in table 5.9.[21] In those results, all groups of movers are compared to those low earners who stayed at their initial jobs for the entire follow-up period (the stay-stayers), so there is a positive earnings difference to be accounted for in each case. The portions of the overall earnings difference accounted for by differences in coefficients and variable means are presented, both overall and for particular characteristics.

The results show that differences across our mobility groups in both mean levels of these characteristics and the market returns to them help to account for overall earnings differences between stay-stayers and those in the other mobility groups. On the one hand, we see that differences in mean levels of tenure detract substantially from the earnings of job-changers relative to those of job-stayers.[22] If we add the differences in the mean numbers of full-quarter earnings—which is essentially a variable measuring nonzero tenure—to those for tenure, the combined differences in means detract even more from the earnings of job-changers. Notably, the losses for those workers who moved earlier and then stayed on their new job are considerably lower than they are for the more recent movers. On the other hand, the higher returns to tenure and especially to full-quarter earnings for all of these groups relative to the persistent job-stayers substantially reduce the total penalty associated with job-changing for these groups. All of this, of course, can be seen in figures 5.2 and 5.3.

We also find that differences in mean firm effects can account for half or more of the earnings differences between job-stayers and recent job-changers, though they account for less of the differences between move-stayers and stay-stayers. When we combine these effects of firms with those that are interacted with job tenure, we get even stronger total effects of job characteristics: they can account for 30 to 40 percent of the higher earnings of move-stayers (relative to perpetual stayers) and nearly all of the higher earnings of the stay-movers.

Table 5.9   Decomposition of Wage Differentials Between Groups of Job-Changers and Job-Stayers, 1999 to 2001

Mobility Group Variable	Stay-Move			Move-Stay			Move-Move		
	(a)	(b)	Total	(a)	(b)	Total	(a)	(b)	Total
Firm effect	29%	58%	62%	−14%	27%	13%	−7%	52%	46%
Tenure	190	−307	−117	99	−76	22	90	−186	-96
Tenure squared	−145	75	−69	−63	23	−41	−48	45	−3
Tenure × firm effect	−29	51	22	1	17	19	−5	33	27
Squared tenure × firm effect	25	−15	9	2	−5	−3	4	-9	-5
Full quarters	116	−15	102	24	−1	23	93	−13	81
Total	202	−103	100	83	17	100	124	−24	100

Source: Authors' compilation.
Note: Shown are the percentages of total wage differentials between each mobility group and "stay-stay" that can be accounted for by: (a) differences in the coefficients and (b) differences in the means of each variable. The decomposition shown in the table is based on the regression specifications in table 5.8. Differences in coefficients are weighted by the means of the own-group variables. Differences in variables are weighted by the coefficients for the stay-stay group.

Thus, the better characteristics of the firms and jobs to which some initial low earners move contribute importantly to their higher labor market earnings despite the costs to them of lower job tenure. Of course, in results not presented in the table, other characteristics of the workers themselves and/or their jobs contribute importantly to earnings differences as well. Overall, differences in regression coefficients—measuring market returns to various characteristics—account for more of the differences in earnings outcomes across mobility groups than do differences in the observed characteristics of people and their jobs.[23]

MORE REGRESSION RESULTS: THE EFFECTS OF EARLY TENURE AND TEMP AGENCIES

The earlier results have clearly demonstrated that, when initial low earners change jobs, the better characteristics of the new jobs and the higher returns to job tenure that they earn contribute importantly to their greater labor market success. On the other hand, prior to changing these jobs, the accumulation of some initial job tenure may help, even in a low-wage job (as the advocates of "work-first" approaches would argue). Early work in a high-wage firm may contribute to higher earnings on another later job as well. The summary results presented here also imply that working with an intermediary, such as a temp agency, is beneficial during this earlier period and may improve workers' access to better employers when they change jobs.

In table 5.10, we present some additional regression results that test these hypotheses. Specifically, we have added some new variables to the regressions for earnings in the 1999 to 2001 period (those presented in table 5.8). These new variables include: whether or not the individual worked for a temp agency earlier; the amount of job tenure they accumulated earlier; and the firm fixed effect in earlier periods.[24]

For those who changed jobs early and then stayed on their new job (move-stayers), we include results from the primary employer during the base period (1993 to 1995). For those who stayed initially on their job and then moved later (stay-movers), we present results from the primary employer during the period 1996 to 1998.[25] And for those who changed employers repeatedly after the base period (move-movers), we include these three variables for the base period, the 1996 to 1998 period, or both. Also, we present results estimated without controlling for the firm effect (first panel) in 1999 to 2001 and also with those controls included (second panel); comparisons across these two sets of results indicate the extent to which any estimated effects associated with earlier work experience matter because they improve the access of low earners to better firms and jobs.[26]

The results show that early accumulation of job tenure and employment with temp agencies both contribute to the subsequent earnings of these individuals after they change jobs, even though the earnings on those initial jobs may be quite low.[27] Specifically, initially working for a temp agency adds 6 to 10 percent to the subsequent earnings of these individuals in the period 1999 to 2001. Additional tenure now has significant positive effects in most cases, though they are relatively small—it adds anywhere from 0.1 to 1 percent to earnings per quarter. Thus, quite a few quarters of early work are needed to generate the same effect as some work with a temp agency. Also, the results indicate that working for a higher-wage firm initially has some longer-term effects as well—perhaps by generating some credentials or training that pays off in subsequent moves to similar jobs.

Furthermore, once we control for the wage premia on current jobs (that is, in the period 1999 to 2001), the impact of working for a temp agency is substantially weakened. This implies that, despite the low wages and benefits they pay, *temp agencies help initial low earners by improving their access to better jobs.* Whether these newer jobs are the same as the ones they worked for while with the temp agencies cannot be determined from these data, but one way or another, experience with a temp agency does seem to improve access. The returns to earlier firm wage premia are also

Table 5.10   Regressions of Log Quarterly Earnings, by Mobility Group with Controls for Base Period Characteristics

	Stay-Move	Move-Stay	Move-Move	Move-Move
Without control for current firm effect				
Fixed firm effect in 1993 to 1995	0.256 (34.36)**	0.378 (35.20)**	0.220 (24.72)**	0.070 (7.87)**
Temp agency in 1993 to 1995	0.103 (8.58)**	0.056 (2.03)*	0.062 (5.33)**	0.000 (0.03)
Tenure in 1993 to 1995	0.001 (1.29)	0.011 (12.08)**	0.006 (8.40)**	0.006 (8.03)**
Fixed firm effect in 1996 to 1998				0.577 (66.60)**
Temp agency in 1996 to 1998				0.099 (8.77)**
Tenure in 1996 to 1998				0.009 (11.47)**
R-squared	0.16	0.13	0.16	0.20
With control for current firm effect				
Fixed firm effect in 1993 to 1995	0.000 (0.05)	0.156 (14.37)**	0.052 (6.20)**	-0.008 (0.93)
Temp agency in 1993 to 1995	0.007 (0.68)	0.014 (0.54)	0.007 (0.70)	-0.016 (1.49)
Tenure in 1993 to 1995	0.004 (6.54)**	0.009 (10.15)**	0.005 (7.73)**	0.005 (7.41)**
Fixed firm effect in 1996 to 1998				0.314 (36.12)**
Temp agency in 1996 to 1998				0.038 (3.51)**
Tenure in 1996 to 1998				0.007 (8.99)**
R-squared	0.32	0.22	0.28	0.29
Observations	77,393	46,086	75,937	75,935

Source: Authors' compilation.
Notes: In addition to the reported coefficients, all specifications include controls for the same variables as in the specification reported in table 5.8. The effects on these variables of the inclusion of base period characteristics are very limited and therefore not reported. Absolute values of t statistics are in parentheses.
*significant at 5 percent; **significant at 1 percent

reduced, but not fully eliminated, by controlling for current wage premia. On the other hand, including controls for quality of firm has little effect on the returns to early job tenure, indicating that early tenure does not improve access to better jobs (though it has other positive effects).

Of course, these results are not based on random assignment or natural experimentation. It is possible that the unmeasured personal characteristics of those who work for temp agencies or those who work for better firms initially and/or gain more early work experience are simply better than those of other low-earning workers. In other words, we may be capturing the "selection" or "creaming" of better workers rather than the causal effects of these factors per se. We have, of course, controlled for person fixed effects in these regressions, so selection on the basis of permanent characteristics can be ruled out. It is possible that temp agencies or better firms are selecting on the basis of some temporary characteristics—such as newly improved attitudes to work—that the fixed effects do not capture. The answers to these questions will have to await other studies based on experimental designs.[28]

Nevertheless, these results do suggest that, even while they have low earnings, the early work experiences of low earners can have positive effects in subsequent jobs. Working with a temp agency, and perhaps with labor market intermediaries more broadly, can improve subsequent access to a good firm and a better-paying job. Working for a better firm today improves an individual's chances of gaining such a job tomorrow, perhaps by providing him or her with transferable occupational skills and/or labor market contacts. And the accumulation of job tenure with any earlier employer has some good long-term effects as well, perhaps through the accumulation of more general skills (such as job-readiness and stability) that can be signaled to other prospective employers. This latter effect, however, is smaller in magnitude than the ones observed for temp agencies and high-wage firms.

CONCLUSIONS

In this chapter, we have addressed the question of whether initial low earners are better served by job *retention* or job *mobility*—that is, by staying on their initial job and accumulating tenure or moving to a new (and perhaps better) job. We have analyzed returns to the accumulation of job tenure in older versus newer jobs for these workers and the levels of and returns to other job characteristics among job-movers versus job-stayers. We have also considered whether the early characteristics of work among job-changers—such as whether they accumulate job tenure or work for a temp agency—have subsequent positive effects after they change jobs, even though their earnings may be quite low at the time.

Our results indicate that, in general, initial low earners who change jobs are more likely to transition out of low earnings than those who stay in their original job. Similarly, most transitions out of low earnings are accounted for by job-changers rather than job-stayers. But the low earners who gain the most in the labor market are those who change jobs early on and then stay in that next job, gaining on-the-job training and accumulating additional job tenure. In general, job-changers are hurt by the loss of some early tenure, though these losses are generally outweighed by the higher returns to tenure in their newer jobs and the higher levels of wages in those jobs more broadly. The higher returns to tenure in higher-wage jobs suggest that both wage growth over time and initial wage levels are enhanced by job changes to higher-wage firms; this implies that workers gain more on-the-job training in such firms and benefit from promotion ladders and other firm policies as well as higher initial wages.

We also find that there is some return to early work experience and tenure before these job changes occur, though the effects of such tenure are fairly small. These findings suggest that "work-first" strategies for low-wage workers have some modest benefits. On the other hand, working for temp agencies—and perhaps labor market intermediaries more broadly—can improve the access of low earners to better firms and higher subsequent earnings. Working for high-wage firms initially also provides some benefits that last beyond a worker's experience with that firm. Taken together, the results imply that *appropriate combinations of early work experience, job training, and mobility across firms can generate the best earnings outcomes for low earners over the long term,* a theme to which we return in chapter 8.

Of course, we emphasize once again that we are not advocating job mobility per se as an answer to the problems of low earners. For one thing, significant costs are associated with job mobility in the form of lost earnings and/or lost job tenure. The literature clearly indicates that some job turnover is counterproductive and generates little (or even negative) earnings growth. The mobility decisions of workers are determined by many personal and job-related factors, and of course sometimes the decision to leave a job is made by the employer (through layoffs and discharges) rather than by the worker (through quits).

But even when workers make their own mobility decisions, these decisions are endogenous with respect to the labor market opportunities that present themselves to them. What we argue is that better labor market opportunities—specifically, better access to higher-wage firms and jobs—

generate the kinds of positive movements across jobs that are associated with transitions out of low earnings for many workers. These jobs provide not only higher initial wages but higher wage growth over time, presumably through on-the-job training.

Exactly how to improve this access is somewhat less clear, though this chapter suggests one possibility: using labor market intermediaries—including temp agencies, among others—to overcome the barriers that low earners (especially minorities) often face in trying to get jobs at better firms.

We explore these and other policy issues in chapter 8. In the meantime, we want to look at a bit more carefully at the firms that hire many low earners and at the geographic locations of these job opportunities.

Chapter Six | Firms That Hire and Advance Low Earners: A Closer Look

THE PRECEDING CHAPTERS have demonstrated that finding the "right" firm can make the difference in a low-wage worker's success or failure in escaping low-wage work. But a major question remains: how can these firms be identified? The evidence presented in the previous chapters provides some guidance: certain firm characteristics, such as industry, firm size, and turnover rate, are all-important indicators of whether a firm provides a pathway to success for low earners. Yet the most important characteristic contributing to a worker's success is the firm's wage premium, or "fixed effect," which is unobservable to local practitioners. Are there other indicators that local service providers might use to identify those that pay high wage premia? There is substantial evidence that such indicators may be available. We know from the literature that different firms within industries organize themselves in very different ways: some, like Nordstrom's, offer substantial opportunities for advancement, while others, like Wal-Mart, do not. Is this true for firms that hire low-wage workers? If so, what are the observable characteristics that are associated with these firms? And how reliable are these characteristics for program planners? Do differences across firms persist over time?

Thus, in this chapter we move from an approach that focuses on individual workers to one that focuses on firms. We try to provide answers to these questions by focusing more specifically on the kinds of firms that hire low earners, as well as on the firms at which such workers succeed over time. We focus on the variation across firms in employment outcomes for low earners not only between industries but also *within* industries. In doing so, we look at the extent to which the hiring and advancement of low earners is concentrated at a small percentage of firms or distributed more broadly within industry groupings. We also analyze the extent to which these characteristics persist over time at the firm level. Finally, we consider whether firms in particular industries are more likely to provide ultimate success themselves or more likely to be stepping-stones to success elsewhere, as well as the extent to which both characteristics vary within and across industries. Ultimately, we hope this analysis leads us to a greater understanding of *why* some firms provide employment and higher earnings to low earners while others do not, even within the same industry.

In analyzing outcomes within industries, we sometimes focus on two industries in more detail—health services and temporary help. There are several reasons for this. The health services industry is both an important employer of low-wage workers and one of the few industries that successfully transition workers out of low-wage work. The choice of the temporary help industry is a natural consequence of the intriguing results uncovered in the previous chapter—that temp agencies appear to help low-wage workers primarily by improving their access to better jobs.

We hope that this chapter can establish some basic knowledge about the way in which different firms, even within the same industry, choose their production approach so that they get very different proportions of low-wage workers, with very different outcomes for the workers who work for them. Eventually this knowledge might be usefully applied to economic development policies to encourage the expansion of firms that offer better opportunities to low earners.

THE CHARACTERISTICS OF FIRMS THAT HIRE LOW-WAGE WORKERS

What kinds of firms hire low-wage workers?[1] Our data permit us to examine this in an unprecedented fashion. Our five-state dataset provides an enormous sample of firms: 1,894,881 firms that hired at least one worker in the 1996 to 1998 period, representing a total of over 74 million hires. In addition, because we have the universe of workers within each firm, we can directly construct firm-level measures of hiring rates and escape rates.

For a sample of prime-age low earners—defined, as before, during the base period 1993 to 1995—we now focus on *the firms that hired these low earners in the period 1996 to 1998.* It is worth noting that only one in three of these firms (561,446 firms) hired at least one prime-age (twenty-five to fifty-four years old) worker with significant labor force attachment (employed at least one quarter in each year) who also had low earnings in the 1993 to 1995 period. We thus end up with a sample of over half a million firms that hired just over 2.4 million low-earning workers in the relevant time period. We also analyze successful transitions (or escapes) from low earnings, either in that period or by the subsequent period, 1999 to 2001. As we did earlier, we focus in each period only on the primary employers of these workers during that time period.

Of course, such a sample omits the low-earning job-stayers who continued to work at the same firms in 1996 to 1998 as in the base period. We know from chapter 5 that the stayers were somewhat older than those who moved and had somewhat lower permanent earnings capacities (as identified by person fixed effects). We also showed in that chapter that the firms that hired the movers paid, on average, higher wage premia than those firms for which they worked previously. Still, given our substantive interest in identifying and analyzing the latter firms, this change of focus seems appropriate. And as we note later in the chapter, at least some of the characteristics of the firms that hired low earners in 1996 to 1998 also apply to those that employed them during the base period.

In creating the firm-level statistics that summarize the outcomes for the low-wage workers these firms hire, we use the same definitions as in the previous chapters. We define a worker as having escaped low earnings, either partially or completely, if he or she moved from being a low earner in 1993 to 1995 to one of the other earnings categories in 1996 to 1998, or especially in 1999 to 2001.

The first striking result on examining this sample—which would not be evident from an examination of worker-based data—is the concentration of hiring. Just one thousand firms hired almost one in four low-wage workers; just ten thousand firms were responsible for hiring almost half of the low-wage workers; and 80 percent of low earners were hired by only one hundred thousand firms. This simple fact could be extremely useful to local practitioners—the search for firms that hire low-wage workers is clearly quite finite.

This concentration can be described in another way: by calculating a ten-firm "concentration ratio" for the hiring of low earners, that is, the proportion of hires accounted for by the most important hiring firms in each industry. We calculate this ratio for each state in our data and provide the range of results in table 6.1.

Although the range varies from state to state, the same pattern is evident. In some industries—especially construction—the concentration of low earners hired is fairly low. But in others the concentration is much greater. For instance, the top ten firms in retail trade (other than eating and drinking establishments) hired about one in four of the low earners hired in that industry; in financial services they hired roughly one-fourth to one-third; and in several other industries (including hotels, personal services,

Table 6.1   The Concentration of Low-Earner Hiring in Selected
Industries, 1996 to 1998

Industry	Range by State
Construction	3.73 to 9.60%
Manufacturing	5.65 to 25.30
Durable goods	13.36 to 100.00
Apparel and other textiles	8.89 to 28.60
Other nondurable goods	14.39 to 24.86
Transportation and utilities	4.29 to 12.94
Wholesale trade	9.20 to 16.80
Retail trade	12.90 to 26.30
Eating and drinking places	14.30 to 27.90
Other retail trade	25.50 to 27.30
Finance, insurance, and real estate	23.70 to 35.40
Services	23.70 to 34.80
Hotels and other lodging places	23.40 to 47.30
Personal services	23.70 to 54.10
Business services	23.70 to 52.80
Help supply services	9.08 to 24.40
Other business services	11.20 to 19.90
Health services	12.70 to 46.40
Education services	6.50 to 27.50
Social services	9.80 to 18.90
Public administration	25.10 to 50.00

Source: Authors' compilation.
Note: These ranges represent the percentages of low earners hired in the industry by the ten
largest firms in each.

and public administration) the ratio gets as high as one-half in some
states. Thus, a simple identification of the top ten hirers of low-wage
workers in a state (or in a local area) often goes a very long way to identify
likely employers of low-wage workers.

Another way of examining this set of facts is to examine the distribution of hiring on a firm-by-firm basis. If we do this by calculating, for each
firm, *the percentages of new hires within firms who are low earners,* we find that
within narrowly defined industries some firms hired no low earners while
others hired only such workers. This is vividly illustrated in figure 6.1,
which graphs the distribution of percentages of hires who were low earners for firms in both the entire economy and temporary help establish-

Figure 6.1   Distribution of Proportion of Hires in 1996 to 1998 Who
Were Low Earners in 1993 to 1995

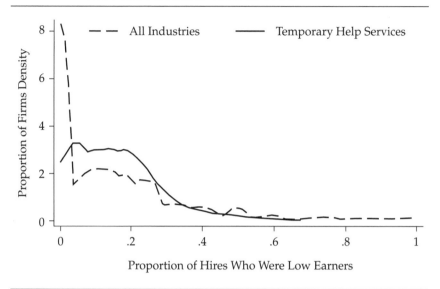

Proportion of Hires Who Were Low Earners

Source: Authors' compilation.
Note: The figure shows Kernel Density Estimates of the distribution of the proportions of
firms' new hires in 1996 to 1998 who were low earners in 1993 to 1995.

ments. While almost half of firms in the economy as a whole hired no low-
wage workers, one-quarter had 20 percent or more low earners in their
hiring pool. And these proportions vary dramatically by industry. In the
temporary help industry, 10 percent of firms hired no low-wage workers
at all, but 80 percent of firms had at least one low-wage worker.[2] Again,
one useful result of this analysis is that it suggests that program planners
can usefully target their efforts at a relatively small subset of firms in key
industries.

Without access to the same microdata, however, service providers need
to have additional information to identify firms that are likely to hire low-
wage workers in a particular industry. When we investigate what accounts for these within-industry differences, we do find some systematic
factors—notably size and turnover rates. If we arbitrarily categorize firms
into three groups—those that have a low proportion of low-wage hires
(under 20 percent), those that have a high proportion (over 80 percent),
and a middle group—there are systematic differences across the firms in
the first two categories. Those firms that hire a high proportion of low-
wage workers are smaller on average (median firm size of nine rather than

Table 6.2   Effects of Firm Characteristics on the Proportions of Low
Earners Hired by Firms

	Proportion of Variation Explained		
Explanatory Variables	Whole Economy	Temporary Help	Health Services
Employment size and turnover	0.01	0.13	0.03
Employment size and turnover plus firm fixed effect	0.10	0.28	0.04
Employment size and turnover plus firm previous hiring proportion	0.17	0.49	0.09

Source: Authors' compilation.
Note: These figures represent R-squared measures from regressions in which the dependent variables were the proportion of all hired workers who were low earners and the explanatory variables are those listed.

nineteen) and have almost twice as much turnover. In addition, these firms have a much lower firm fixed effect than do those that hire a low proportion of low-wage workers. This firm-level analysis directly corresponds to the worker-level analysis in the earlier chapters.

However, this analysis does not go a very long way to identifying which firms are likely to hire low earners—the first order of business for targeting placement services. Table 6.2 presents evidence on the proportions of the variation in fractions of new hires who are low earners explained (R-squared) in regression equations that include a variety of firm characteristics as independent variables. The table shows that if service providers simply use employment size and turnover to identify firms that are likely to hire low earners, their placement success will improve by only about 1 percent relative to random chance. If they target particular industries, however, the odds of placement are better—for example, using size and turnover improves the chances of success by about 13 percent in temporary help services, although only by about 3 percent in health services. Being able to identify the firm fixed effects would substantially increase service providers' chances of success—tenfold for the economy as a whole, and more than doubling their odds in temporary help placements—though these are generally not observable to service providers.

Fortunately, there are other indicators that can be used. As discussed in the opening section of this chapter, economic analysis suggests that firms do not randomly choose workers. Instead, the demand for less-skilled workers at any firm is likely to be a systematic outcome of the way in which the firm chooses to organize its production; hence, the hiring patterns of low earners at firms should be persistent over time. Indeed, when

Figure 6.2   Firm-Level Persistence in Proportion of New Hires Who
Were Low Earners in the Preceding Three-Year Period

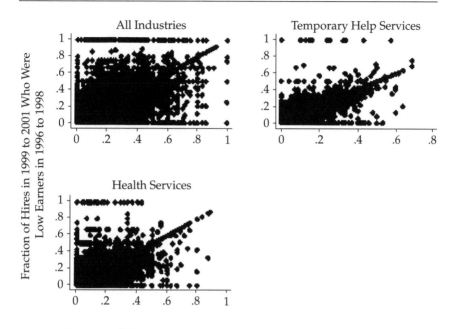

Fraction of Hires in 1996 to 1998 Who Were Low Earners in 1993 to 1995

Source: Authors' compilation.

the proportions of low earners hired in the previous period by the same firms are added to the set of explanatory variables, the variation in hiring outcomes rises substantially.

To further investigate this possibility of using firms' previous hiring patterns as an observable factor to help predict current hiring patterns, we calculated the proportion of hires for each firm in 1999 to 2001 who were low earners in the period 1996 to 1998, as well as the proportion of all hires in 1996 to 1998 who were low earners in 1993 to 1995; we then plotted them against each other in figure 6.2. The first graph shows the relationship between prior and current hires for all firms in the economy, and the other two graphs show the same for the two narrowly defined low-wage industries we are particularly interested in—temporary help services and health and medical services.

In examining the first graph, we see a striking difference in firms' hiring of low-wage workers. Some firms hire 100 percent low-wage workers, some 0 percent, and the proportion varies all along the spectrum. And there appears to be substantial persistence: firms that hired 0 percent low-wage workers in 1993 to 1995 were likely to hire a very low proportion of low-wage workers in 1996 to 1998; those that hired high proportions in 1993 to 1995 were likely to hire high proportions in 1996 to 1998, as evidenced by the clustering of observations along the forty-five-degree line. This suggests that firms do indeed choose very different hiring strategies and that these are deliberate rather than random. As a result, prior hiring patterns are likely to be good predictors of future hiring behavior.

Obviously these differences could reflect industry-specific patterns, so we examine the same relationships in the temporary help services and health and medical services industries. We find a very similar pattern: some firms within each of these narrowly defined industries persistently hire low proportions of low-wage workers; others persistently hire high proportions.

And when we estimate the direct relationship between these outcomes over time, we find that firms' previous hiring patterns are excellent predictors of current hiring. As the results in the last row of table 6.1 indicate, we can explain about 17 percent of the variation in low-wage hiring in the economy as a whole—and as much as 49 percent of the variation in firm-level hiring of these workers in the temporary help services—by including the past hiring of low earners among the explanatory variables in these regressions.

These findings strongly indicate that firms, even within narrowly defined industries, do choose different hiring strategies. Moreover, these strategies are clearly deliberate—the proportion of low earners hired in one period is highly correlated with the proportion hired three years later. This finding, which is of use in its own right for placement purposes, now leads us to the next section: identifying the characteristics of the firms that are most likely to enable workers to escape low earnings over time.

THE FIRM CHARACTERISTICS ASSOCIATED WITH ESCAPE FROM LOW EARNINGS

Although it is important to find firms that are likely to *hire* low-wage workers, it is even more important to find firms that are likely to facilitate their *escape* from low-wage status. Our earlier chapters found that an important firm characteristic was the industry in which a worker worked: low-earning workers were much more likely to escape low earnings if they worked in some industries than in others. In this section, we expand on this finding and also identify other firm characteristics that increase the likelihood of escape.[3]

How important is industry as a firm characteristic? Our analysis suggests that it is very important. The top ten low-wage industries in 1996 to 1998 accounted for 34 percent of workers who fully escaped low-earning status by the period 1999 to 2001.[4] Furthermore, when we calculate the *proportions* of those hired low earners who escaped this status—rather than simply the *numbers* who escaped—we find substantial variation in success rates across industries. Not surprisingly, only 7 percent of those hired into retail trade fully escaped, compared with 27 percent of those hired into public administration. Although the reasons for these differences across industries are not discernible from the raw data, they probably reflect differences in their average wage premia as well as in training and human resource practices more broadly.

However, as with hiring patterns, industry classification is not a perfect predictor of successful transitions out of low earnings—the marked differences across industries in these success rates are matched by heterogeneity within industries. Focusing on the two examples of interest—the health services industry and the temporary help industry—figure 6.3 plots the proportions of those low earners hired by any firm in 1996 to 1998 who escaped low earnings by the period 1999 to 2001.[5]

Clearly, most firms in the health services industry that hire low earners do not provide escape from this status; indeed, in the modal firm in the industry no workers escaped low-earning status. However, the second mode in health services represents firms that enabled *all* low earners in the industry to escape, and there are relatively few firms in between. By contrast, escape rates in temporary help firms are somewhat evenly distributed across firms. Indeed, in about 40 percent of firms in temporary help services more than half of the low-wage hires escaped low-wage status, while fewer than 10 percent of health services firms achieved the same success rate. But in both cases the heterogeneity in escape rates for low earners hired across firms within the same industries is substantial.

This heterogeneity makes the task of identifying firms that provide successful transitions out of low-wage work simpler—simply because such firms are relatively scarce. As before, just a few large firms did much of the hiring, and just a few account for the preponderance of workers who escaped low-wage status. For example, of the 22,326 health services firms in Florida, only slightly over 6,000 firms ever hired a low-earning worker, and just 20 firms accounted for over 10 percent of all complete escapes out of low earnings. In Maryland, of some 6,000 health services firms, fewer than 2,000 hired a low-earning worker, and just 20 firms accounted for 24 percent of all complete escapes in that industry.

Just as in the previous section, this heterogeneity in success rates across firms leads us to ask: can past behavior, such as the previous success rate

Figure 6.3   Distribution of Proportions of Low-Earning Hires in
              Temporary Help and Health Services in 1996 to 1998
              Who Escaped That Status

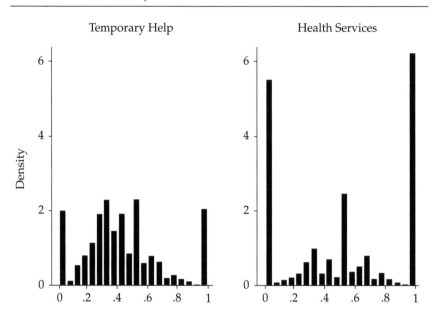

Proportion of Low-Wage Hires in 1996 to 1998 Who Escaped in 1996 to 1998

Source: Authors' compilation.

of low-wage hires in escaping poverty, also be used to predict future outcome? In figure 6.4, the two graphs for our two industries[6] plot the escape
rates for low earners hired in each firm in 1999 to 2001 against the escape
rates at the same firms among those hired in 1996 to 1998.[7] We find the
same wide variation in escape rates that were evident in the earlier
figure—and the same remarkable persistence in a firm's ability to provide
jobs that permit workers to escape low-earning status.

Table 6.3 summarizes precisely how much firm-level information can
be used to identify these "good" firms. It is similar to table 6.2 in that it
provides the proportions of variations of hiring outcomes across firms accounted for by firm characteristics, but in this case the outcome is the proportion of low earners who escaped that status by 1999 to 2001. The first
row shows that employment size and turnover certainly improve the odds
better than chance, but not in a compelling fashion. Including the firm

Figure 6.4   Firm-Level Persistence in Escape Rates: Fraction of Newly
Hired Low Earners Who Escaped Low Earnings in
1996 to 1998 Versus 1999 to 2001

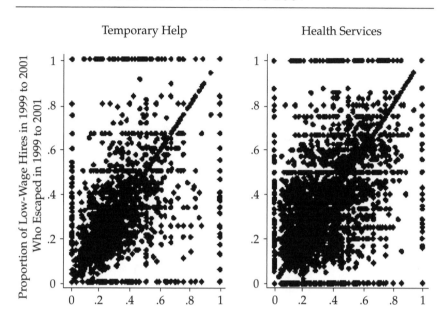

Proportion of Low-Wage Hires in 1996 to 1998 Who Escaped in 1996 to 1998

Source: Authors' compilation.

Table 6.3   Effects of Firm Characteristics on the Proportions of Low
Earners Hired by Firms

| | Proportion of Variation Explained | | |
Explanatory Variables	Whole Economy	Temporary Help	Health Services
Employment size and turnover	0.05	0.01	0.06
Employment size and turnover plus firm fixed effect	0.12	0.1	0.14
Employment size and turnover plus firm escape rate	0.15	0.19	0.18

Source: Authors' compilation.
Note: Results are based on firms that hired at least five low earners in the 1996 to 1998 period.

fixed effect improves the odds substantially, and the firm previous hiring strategy even more so. The results of this exercise are startlingly similar to those presented in the previous section.

Once again, we find that firms are very different in the proportions of their hired low earners who ultimately escape; this difference is clearly heavily driven by industry, but it is also very different within industries. Moreover, the outcomes are not random: there is substantial evidence that these differences persist over time. In sum, how low-wage workers have fared in a firm in a previous period is a strong predictor of how low-wage hires will fare in subsequent periods.

In concrete terms, these results have two implications that could be useful guides for research and policy. The first is that resources could usefully be allocated to identifying firms in the local community that have hired low earners in the past and put them on the path to success. The second is that researchers need to develop an understanding of why different firms within each industry choose such different personnel strategies; perhaps policymakers could then develop strategies that encourage more firms to pay higher wages and have the appropriate human resources policies that accompany these practices, as we discuss in chapter 8.

HOW SOME FIRMS ENABLE WORKERS TO ESCAPE LOW-WAGE STATUS

Differences across firms in rates of escape are clearly important. But a major question remains: how and when do firms enable workers to escape low-wage status? In previous chapters, we have found substantial differences in these pathways: some workers escape by staying with the same firm and others do so by moving to new firms. In this section, we investigate this issue further by analyzing the extent to which those who moved once and ultimately escaped low earnings remained with the same new firm or moved to other ones.

Our measure of each firm's ability to enable workers to escape low-wage status and stay within the firm is defined as the fraction of low earners hired in 1996 to 1998 who still worked for the same firm in 1999 to 2001 and had escaped low earnings (partially or completely) by that time. The measure of each firm's ability to advance low earners in subsequent jobs is defined as the fraction of low earners who worked for a different firm in 1999 to 2001 from the one that hired them in 1996 to 1998, but who had escaped low earnings by 1999 to 2001.

Of course, in the latter case it is possible for a worker's escape to have occurred either in the earlier period (at the first firm that hired him or her after the base period) or in the later one (at the second firm only). We provide some evidence on this here as well; either way, however, we infer that the firm that hired the low earner in 1996 to 1998 had some positive effects on the ultimate earnings outcomes observed for those low earners.

We examine industry differences in two ways. We first calculate, for each industry, the success rate represented by staying with the firm—the average proportion of low-wage hires at firms who had escaped by 1999 to 2001 and who stayed with the firm.[8] We also calculate the success rate associated with firm mobility—the average proportion of workers hired by each firm who escaped and were no longer with the firm in the subsequent period.[9] Figure 6.5 plots, by industry, these two different pathways associated with success. If an industry is in the top right quadrant, this shows that the typical firm in the industry has a higher proportion of workers who escaped both ways; in the bottom right, a higher proportion escaped through mobility than by staying at the firm. Similarly, the typical firm in an industry in the top left quadrant is more likely than the average to offer low earners a pathway to success by staying with the firm, and firms in the bottom left quadrant are less likely than average to offer either.

The clearest result that emerges from figure 6.5 is a fairly strong positive correlation between the two paths to success; in other words, industries that offer successful options to job-stayers often provide them to job-movers as well. This is consistent with what we observed in chapter 5—namely, that employment at firms that paid high wage premia in the past is often associated with greater success for low earners in the present, even at different firms. Perhaps this is due to the package of human resource policies often associated with higher-wage firms, such as more investment in on-the-job training and the like. In this analysis, it is clear that the bottom left quadrant contains the same sets of industries that were identified earlier as offering relatively few prospects for escaping low earnings: retail trade (especially eating and drinking establishments) and personal services. In the upper right quadrant, the leading industries to offer both types of pathways out of low-wage work are health services, financial services, and transportation and utilities.

But there are also some interesting cases of industries offering more of one path to success than the other. For example, the typical firm in temporary help services offers low earners an above-average probability of exiting low-wage status if they change firms, but almost no chance if they stay with the firm. As we noted earlier, temp agencies seem to offer low earners better access to other higher-wage firms rather than higher-wage employment at the agency itself. In contrast, the typical entity in public administration offers a very strong within-firm career pathway, but the prospects for workers who switch entities are not as great. The manufacturing industries also tend to offer a better than average chance of escape

Figure 6.5   Across-Industry Differences in Pathways Out of
Low-Wage Work

Across-Industry Differences in Typical Pathways

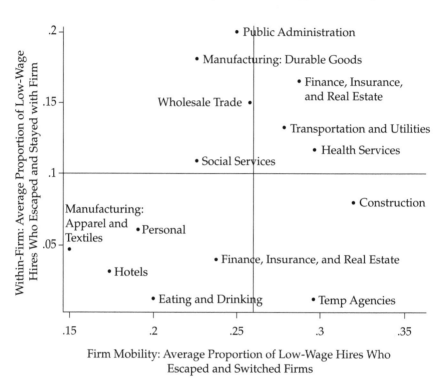

Firm Mobility: Average Proportion of Low-Wage Hires Who
Escaped and Switched Firms

Source: Authors' compilation.

if workers stay with the firm, but lower than average success as a result of firm mobility. Employment in these industries seems less likely to offer successful pathways elsewhere, perhaps because the relatively high wages they pay are associated with less training or with skills that are less general and transferable to other industries.

Of course, these results provide only cross-industry comparisons; one of the strengths of the firm-level analysis in this chapter is the ability to focus on within-industry differences as well. Thus, we calculate—again within each industry—the variation (the standard deviation) in the proportion of workers who escape in each firm by means of the two different pathways. We standardize this by dividing by the mean (the coefficient of

Figure 6.6   Within-Industry Differences in Pathways Out of Low-Wage Work

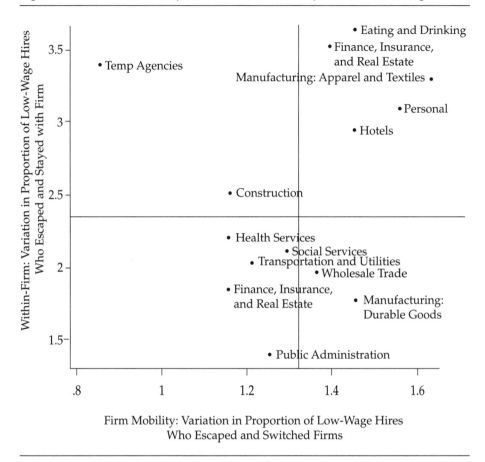

variation), and we note that no variation at all would be reflected in a measure of zero, while greater variation is measured by larger values of this statistic.

Figure 6.6 gives us a sense of the within-industry variation in these two pathways relative to the overall variation in the economy. Again, the four quadrants reflect above- and below-average heterogeneity in variation: there is much less firm-level variation in outcomes for workers in industries that are closer to the origin; more variation along both dimensions in the upper right quadrant; less variation along both dimensions in the lower left quadrant; and so on. From a service provider's point of view, this figure gives an indication of how "good" an indicator industry is in terms of permitting escape through the two pathways—or, on the other hand, how likely it is that there are substantial differences in worker experience across firms within the same industry.

The results show, once again, a strong positive correlation between the two measures of variation across industries. Among the industries with the greatest variation across firms in either form of advance are eating and drinking establishments, hotels, apparel and textiles, and personal services. Their position in the top right quadrant suggests that some firms are highly likely to provide both means of escape, while other firms are much less likely to do so. In these cases, not much precision is provided by knowledge of these particular industries. By contrast, the variation across firms within the temporary help services industry is remarkably low on the firm-changing dimension, but very high on the within-firm dimension. This makes sense, since temp agencies often generate successful matches for these workers with other firms but not with their own. Health services, financial services, and public administration firms consistently show nearly average amounts of variation across firms along both dimensions of success.

Finally, we return to the issue of *when* (and with which employer) the escape occurred for low earners who had successfully transitioned out of this status by 1999 to 2001 and who had changed employers again across the two time periods in question. If the successful escape occurred later, then the intervening firm might be considered a stepping-stone to success (by providing appropriate work experience and/or training), while, if it occurred earlier, the initial employer after the base period probably contributed to this success more directly.

Our results generally indicate that, depending on the industry, the transitions occur at the intervening firms roughly half of the time. In the higher-wage sectors (such as construction, durable manufacturing, transportation and utilities, financial services, and public administration), the escapes from low earnings are more likely to occur right away; in the lower-wage sectors (such as retail trade, apparel and textiles, personal service, and temp agencies), the escapes more frequently occur with the subsequent employer.[10] Even in these latter sectors, employment experience can provide a stepping-stone to ultimate success.

CONCLUSIONS

In this chapter, we show that many firms hire low earners, though fairly large portions of the hiring are concentrated in small numbers of firms in each industry. Furthermore, a substantial fraction of firms regularly provide low-wage workers with pathways out of low-wage work. The rates of hiring and success systematically vary across industry—since some are more highly unionized, more concentrated, or more likely to have production processes that offer many promotion possibilities—but there is a remarkable amount of within-industry variation in firm practices as well.

This chapter has identified a number of characteristics that are associated with firms offering good opportunities to low-wage workers and that could be used by local service providers to help sort out many of these differences. Besides industry, we find here (as we did in earlier chapters) that firm size and turnover rates are associated with escape rates for low earners. But more importantly, this chapter also shows that both the hiring and escape rates of low earners across firms persist over time. Thus, knowing something about a firm's past practices can give an important indication of current and future opportunities for low earners at that firm. Some firms and industries seem to work as stepping-stones to future employment success elsewhere, while others contribute to these outcomes more quickly and directly.

The chapter also raises intriguing long-run questions about within-industry heterogeneity in the outcomes observed across firms. Why do some firms choose a "high road," or high-wage approach, to production, while others choose a low-wage approach? Many important policy implications hinge on finding the answer to this question, as we discuss in chapter 8. In the meantime, and despite some recent advances, a good deal more remains to be learned about these firm choices.

Chapter Seven | Where Are the Good Jobs? The Role of Local Geography

SEVERAL KEY THEMES have emerged from the earlier chapters. Low-wage workers are highly concentrated in particular types of firms and industries. Different demographic groups have differential access to firms that pay high wages, and this has important consequences for their ability to exit low-wage work. But what determines differential access? One possibility is that low-earning workers live farther away from where the high-wage jobs are located and have difficulty reaching them.

Once again, this is a possibility we can examine because of the richness of the LEHD data, which includes information on where workers live and work. We carry out most of the analysis combining data from three states (California, Illinois, and Minnesota), but we focus on single states and particular metropolitan areas within those states for some of the analysis.

We use these data to examine whether where workers live affects the jobs they are able to get and the effect on their earnings. In keeping with the dynamic analysis of chapters 4 and 5, we also ask whether and how much the nature of location matters in escaping low pay.

We present a number of basic empirical findings about the relationships between residential locations of low earners, escapes from this status, locations of high-wage premium jobs, and commute distances. First, we establish that low earners were generally located farther away from the "good jobs" than were nonlow earners. Second, we show that this greater distance to higher-wage jobs was not counteracted by longer commuting by low earners. Indeed, low earners tended to commute shorter distances than nonlow earners. Third, we show a strong negative correlation across counties and census tracts between the fractions of low-wage workers living there and average job quality. This suggests that location appears to matter for access to good jobs. Fourth, we take a dynamic perspective and show that workers were more likely to escape low earnings if they lived near better jobs and/or commuted longer distances.

Not all of these findings are new, and the strong correlations we present here do not necessarily prove causal relationships between geographic factors and employment outcomes of low earners. But we interpret these findings as strongly suggesting some causal link between the two. A lengthy literature on "spatial mismatch" between employment opportunities and the residences of low-income workers, especially for minorities and welfare recipients, already exists (see, for example, Ihlanfeldt and Sjoquist 1998; Stoll, Holzer, and Ihlanfeldt 2000; Allard and Danziger 2003). Our results here are consistent with that literature and suggest that local geographic factors may limit access to higher-wage jobs for low earners more broadly.

Before we set out on the analysis, however, we define the spatial data we use.

DEFINING THE LOCAL GEOGRAPHY

Parts of the analysis in this chapter are quite computationally burdensome; therefore, we restrict the sample to three states only—California, Illinois, and Minnesota—and three metropolitan areas within these states: Los Angeles, Chicago, and the Twin City area (Minneapolis and St. Paul).[1] The establishments and workers in these states have been geocoded on a latitude and longitude basis using internal census mapping software.[2] Data on the locations of business are available on a quarterly basis from the beginning of the 1990s, but workers' residence data are available only on an annual basis for the most recent years. Thus, while our ability to study the geographical dimensions of job dynamics is quite good, our ability to study the dynamics in workers' places of residence is more limited.

One limitation of the data is that there are no direct geographic data links between workers and *establishments* but only between workers and *firms* in the LEHD data. Thus, we do not know with certainty in which particular establishment a worker was employed if the employing firm consisted of more than one establishment, which was true of about 30 percent of our workforce. In the Minnesota data, however, direct links between workers and establishments (rather than firms) are available. In data for the other states, we use probabilistic links between workers and establishments that have been calculated in the LEHD data.[3] We have also verified—by comparing our results with those obtained from subsamples in which direct links between workers and firms are available (that is, in the Minnesota data and for workers employed in single-establishment firms in all three states)—that the statistical properties of the probabilistic links do not affect our results.

To characterize the geographical dimensions of the labor market, we calculate commuting distances and measures of the quality of locally available jobs for each worker in the year 2000. Commuting distance is simply the straight-line distance (in miles) between the geographical co-ordinates of the worker's place of residence and the location of the worker's primary employer during the year.

We characterize the quality of the workers' local jobs in terms of the wage premia paid by employers close to where the workers resided. In particular, for each worker we calculate the employment-weighted aver-age of the estimated firm wage premia of all firms located within concen-tric circles defined by two-, five-, and ten-mile radii around the geograph-ical coordinates of the worker's place of residence. These measures can be interpreted as the firm-wage premia a worker could expect if randomly matched with an employer in these areas.

Finally, we use the same definition of low earners as in the previous chapters: workers who were twenty-five to fifty-four years old and who each year reported earnings of at least $2,000 but consistently below $12,000 over a consecutive three-year period.

THE CHARACTERISTICS OF NEIGHBORHOODS: WHERE LOW-WAGE WORKERS AND HIGH-WAGE JOBS ARE LOCATED

We start by exploring where workers with low earnings in 1999 to 2001 lived and whether there was substantial geographic variation in the con-centration of low-wage workers and high-wage jobs. We focus on Califor-nia for this analysis.[4] For the entire state, we calculate what proportions of workers who lived in each census tract were low earners. We graph the distribution of these proportions for the entire state in figure 7.1. We find that, of the almost seven thousand tracts in California, over five thousand had fewer than 20 percent of their residents defined as low earners, but in over seventy tracts more than 40 percent of residents were low earners. And those tracts that had high concentrations of low earners were not ran-domly scattered across the state but in fact were often located quite close to each other, as is evident from the map in figure 7.2.

Looking at the geographic concentration from another angle, we map the location of high-wage jobs, defined as jobs with a firm-wage premium in the upper quartile for the state. Figure 7.3 shows the distribution of these jobs within census tracts, and figure 7.4 presents the map of these

Figure 7.1   Distribution of Fraction of Low-Wage Workers Across
             Census Tracts in California

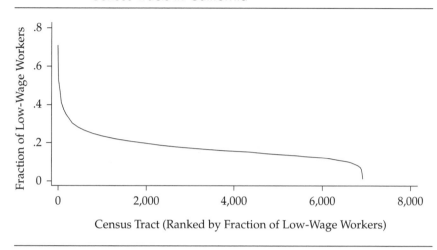

Figure 7.2   Fraction of Low Earners in Census Tract Populations in California

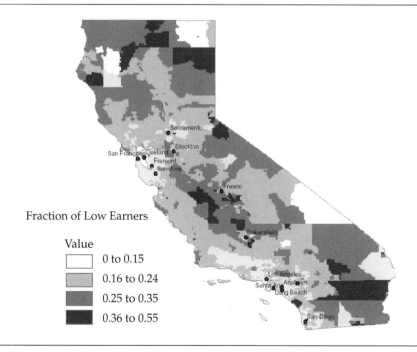

Figure 7.3   Distribution of Fraction of High-Wage Jobs Across Census Tracts in California

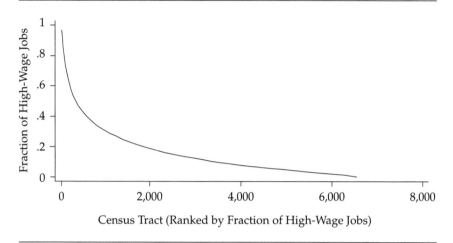

Source: Authors' compilation.

Figure 7.4   Fraction of High-Wage Jobs in Each Census Tract in California

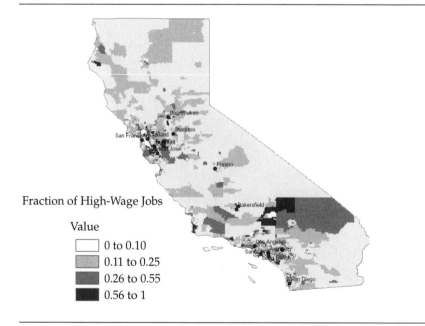

Source: Authors' compilation.

jobs for California. It is clear that most of the high-wage jobs were located in or near the major urban centers; Silicon Valley can also be identified. In a small number of tracts almost all jobs were high-wage jobs, but in over 4,500 tracts fewer than 20 percent of all jobs paid high wage premia. A glance at the two maps suggests that the low-earning workers and the high-wage jobs were generally in different places within the state.

We repeat this exercise for a single (though very large) urban county in California: Los Angeles County. The equivalent displays are in figures 7.5 through 7.8. Figure 7.5 shows the same pattern as for the statewide distribution—a small number of tracts had high concentrations of low earners. Figure 7.6 again shows that areas of high low-wage worker density were often contiguous. Similarly, figures 7.7 and 7.8 show the same sort of distribution for high-wage jobs as in the statewide graphs. Again, the maps suggest that low earners and high-wage jobs were typically located in different parts of the county.

Furthermore, when we analyze data on blacks and Hispanics in Los Angeles County (who are either low earners or nonlow earners), we find that their residences were disproportionately concentrated among low earners and/or those with low personal fixed effects. They were not necessarily farther away from the areas where high-wage jobs were found, though some other analyses find that they were farther away from areas of job *growth* and from high-wage jobs in some key industries (such as construction and manufacturing) (for more evidence on this issue, see

Figure 7.5   Distribution of Fraction of Low-Wage Workers Across Census Tracts in Los Angeles County

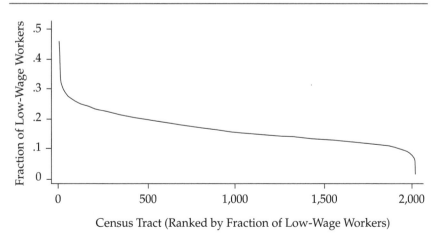

Source: Authors' compilation.

Figure 7.6   Fraction of Low Earners in Census Tract Populations in Los
Angeles County

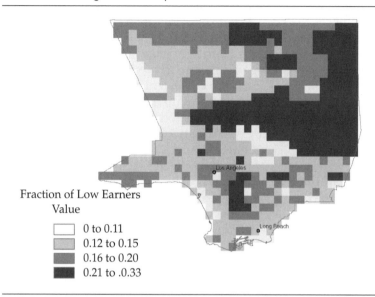

Source: Authors' compilation.

Figure 7.7   Distribution of Fraction of High-Wage Jobs Across Census
Tracts in Los Angeles County

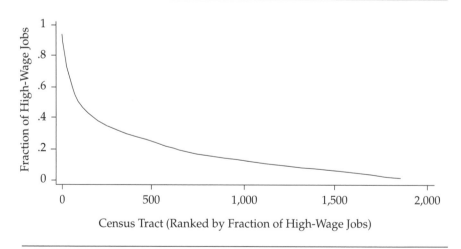

Source: Authors' compilation.

Figure 7.8   Fraction of High-Wage Jobs in Each Census Tract in
Los Angeles County

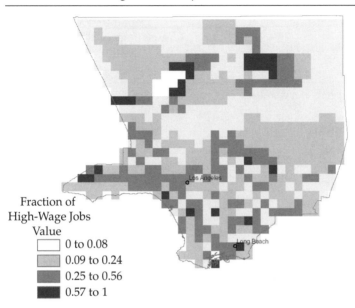

Fraction of
High-Wage Jobs
Value
☐ 0 to 0.08
▨ 0.09 to 0.24
▨ 0.25 to 0.56
■ 0.57 to 1

Source: Authors' compilation.

Raphael 1998; Stoll, Holzer, and Ihlanfeldt 2000; Johnson 2002; Andersson, Holzer, and Lane 2003).

The figures and maps display the concentration of low earners and high-wage jobs in California. Using regression analysis, we examine the relationship between high-wage job location and the presence of low earners across all three states. To be precise, we ask how much of the spatial variation in the prevalence of low earnings can be accounted for by the variation in the quality of locally available jobs.

Table 7.1 presents these regression results. We simply regress the fraction of low earners who resided in each tract (county) on the mean quality of jobs (wage premia) in each census tract (or county).

The first thing to note in table 7.1 is the explanatory power of the simple regressions. The variation in average firm wage markups across tracts (counties) accounts for 35 percent (30 percent) of the variation in the fraction of low earners. Second, note the very strong *negative* relationship between the location of high-wage jobs and the presence of low earners. This finding confirms the visual impression gained from the maps in figures

Table 7.1   Impact of Firm Wage Premia on Fractions of Local
Residents Who Are Low Earners

	Dependent Variable: Percentage of Residents Who Are Low Earners in	
	Tract	County
Mean firm wage premia in county	−0.243 (0.010)**	−0.265 (0.033)**
Mean firm wage premia in tract	−0.236 (0.004)**	
R-squared	0.346	0.302
Observations	6,124	181

Source: Authors' compilation.
**significant at 1 percent

7.2, 7.4, 7.6, and 7.8. The quality of locally available jobs is significantly and negatively correlated with the fraction of workers who had low earnings; furthermore, variations across space in job quality account for a substantial fraction of variations in low earnings status.

LOCAL LABOR MARKETS AND COMMUTING

This mismatch between where low earners live and where high-wage jobs are located has two potential impacts. First, it may be that low earners do get good jobs but have to travel a lot farther to get them. Second, it may be that low earners simply do not get the good jobs. We consider the first of these possibilities in this section, and the second in the next.

Table 7.2 presents the distribution of commuting distances for the three states, separately for low earners and nonlow earners.[5] We also differentiate between the whole state and the three metro areas on which we focus (Los Angeles County, the Twin Cities area, and Cook County).

The strongest result is that low earners were much more likely to work close to where they lived. Consider the results for Los Angeles County. Almost half (46 percent) of all low earners commuted less than five miles, compared to just over one-quarter (27 percent) of nonlow earners. Conversely, 45 percent of nonlow earners commuted over ten miles, compared to 30 percent of low earners. This pattern was repeated across the whole state of California, and also across the other states. Residents of the Twin Cities area had fewer long commutes overall, but there is still a striking

Table 7.2   Distribution of Commuting Distances, by Area and Earnings Category

Area	Earnings Category	Under Five Miles	Five to Ten Miles	Eleven to Twenty-Five Miles	Twenty-Six to Fifty Miles	All
California	Low earners	0.47	0.23	0.22	0.08	1.00
	Nonlow earners	0.30	0.25	0.32	0.13	1.00
Illinois	Low earners	0.53	0.21	0.19	0.07	1.00
	Nonlow earners	0.33	0.24	0.33	0.10	1.00
Minnesota	Low earners	0.52	0.21	0.22	0.06	1.00
	Nonlow earners	0.34	0.25	0.34	0.07	1.00
Los Angeles County, California	Low earners	0.46	0.24	0.24	0.06	1.00
	Nonlow earners	0.28	0.26	0.36	0.11	1.00
Cook County, Illinois	Low earners	0.47	0.25	0.22	0.05	1.00
	Nonlow earners	0.29	0.29	0.36	0.06	1.00
Twin City area, Minnesota	Low earners	0.48	0.28	0.23	0.02	1.00
	Nonlow earners	0.35	0.34	0.30	0.01	1.00

Source: Authors' compilation.

difference between the patterns for low earners and nonlow earners: 48 percent of low earners traveled less than five miles, compared to 35 percent of nonlow earners.

Focusing on California, table 7.3 reports detailed commuting patterns by demographic group. Among low earners, there is a significant difference between the commute distances of men and women: higher fractions of women commuted short distances. Over 50 percent of white women commuted less than five miles, compared to 42 percent of white men; comparable results are 48 percent and 40 percent among Hispanics and a smaller difference among Asians and blacks. The male-female difference is less marked among nonlow earners.

Another noteworthy result is that black men and women had strikingly longer commute distances than whites. Among low earners, 38 percent of black women commuted less than five miles, compared to 52 percent of white women, and only 33 percent of black men did so, compared to 42 percent of white men. Again, the differences are smaller among nonlow earners. But this result conflicts somewhat with earlier evidence, showing that young blacks spent more time commuting (because of their lower rates of car ownership) but sometimes covered shorter distances.[6]

Table 7.3 Distribution of Commuting Distances in California, by Earnings Category and Demographic Group

	Low Earners					Nonlow Earners				
	Under Five Miles	Five to Ten Miles	Eleven to Twenty-Five Miles	Twenty-Six to Fifty Miles	All	Under Five Miles	Five to Ten Miles	Eleven to Twenty-Five Miles	Twenty-Six to Fifty Miles	All
All	0.47	0.23	0.22	0.08	1.00	0.30	0.25	0.32	0.13	1.00
By demographic group										
White female	0.52	0.21	0.19	0.07	1.00	0.34	0.25	0.30	0.10	1.00
Black female	0.38	0.29	0.24	0.09	1.00	0.27	0.28	0.33	0.11	1.00
Asian female	0.52	0.23	0.19	0.06	1.00	0.29	0.28	0.33	0.09	1.00
Hispanic female	0.48	0.24	0.21	0.07	1.00	0.34	0.26	0.30	0.10	1.00
White male	0.42	0.23	0.25	0.10	1.00	0.27	0.23	0.34	0.16	1.00
Black male	0.33	0.26	0.29	0.12	1.00	0.24	0.26	0.34	0.16	1.00
Asian male	0.48	0.23	0.22	0.06	1.00	0.26	0.27	0.36	0.11	1.00
Hispanic male	0.41	0.25	0.25	0.09	1.00	0.32	0.25	0.31	0.12	1.00

Source: Authors' compilation.

The overall commuting results combined with earlier results create something of a puzzle. If nonlow earners lived closer to high-wage jobs than did low earners, why did they commute even farther? The answers to this question may be found in the broader literature in urban economics on choice of residence and commutes. For instance, the income elasticity of preferences for suburban amenities appears to be greater than one; thus, higher-income families often choose to live farther away from downtown job areas and to commute longer distances (Mieszkowski and Mills 1993). Another reason for the longer commutes of nonlow earners may be the tendency of more highly educated workers to operate in labor markets that are wider in geographic scope, perhaps because of their more specialized skills or because of their greater information about job opportunities. Their tendency to live closer to high-wage jobs may have more to do with where high-wage *employers* choose to locate than with the high earners themselves, who often do not work at these nearby jobs.

Does this analysis thus imply that spatial factors do not matter for low earners? Not necessarily. Minorities and/or the poor may be constrained in their housing choices by housing market discrimination (Yinger 1995) or by the high cost of housing in desirable neighborhoods. If they are also limited in their ability to commute by lack of private auto transportation, limited public transit options, or a lack of information about dispersed job opportunities, their access to good jobs will be limited as well.

Furthermore, our empirical analysis suggests that the consequence of low-wage workers living far from the good jobs is not resolved by their commuting a long way. Even though our data show that black low earners commuted considerably farther than white low earners, they still commuted shorter distances than black nonlow earners. We return to this difference later in the chapter. In the meantime, it seems quite possible that the poor geographical residential locations of low earners limit the quality of the jobs that they take. We provide more evidence on the geography and commutes of low earners in the next section.

LOCAL LABOR MARKETS AND ESCAPE FROM LOW-WAGE STATUS

We have shown that there is an important negative correlation between the quality of locally available jobs and the prevalence of low earners across geographic areas. The next step is to look at the influence of local employer quality on the probability that a low earner will escape this status.

We present the results in this section in two ways. First, we revisit commute patterns for workers who had low earnings in 1996 to 1998 in light of their earnings transition status in 1999 to 2001, both in summary statistics and in the context of regression analysis. Second, we estimate the relationship between the quality of locally available jobs and probabilities of escaping low earnings.

Table 7.4 shows that initial low earners who escaped their earnings status (those workers with low earnings in 1996 to 1998 and nonlow earnings in 1999 to 2001) had longer commutes in 2000 than non-escapers (those workers with low earnings in both periods). While only 27 percent of non-escapers commuted over ten miles, 38 percent of escapers traveled that far. Similarly, half of non-escapers commuted only within five miles, compared to 37 percent of escapers. The patterns by demographic group mirror those of table 7.2. For example, there is a big difference in the percentages of those who commuted over ten miles between white female escapers (35 percent) and white female non-escapers (24 percent), and a higher level and smaller gap for black females (38 percent of escapers and 30 percent of non-escapers). The clear pattern across all groups is that low earners who escaped their earnings status commuted farther than those who remained low earners.

However, we need to be cautious about directly interpreting this to mean that some workers escaped low earnings status by seeking and winning jobs farther from their homes—that is, by commuting for longer distances. At a minimum, we need to control for individual characteristics that might also influence these outcomes. We do this in table 7.5. The table presents odds ratios from logistic regressions in which the probability of escape is regressed on commute times, controlling for person fixed effects and residence in metropolitan areas.[7]

These results suggest that individuals with high person fixed effects (which probably reflect their higher skills or other personal qualities) were more likely to leave low-earning status and that living in a metro area reduced the chances of escape. Turning to the commute variables, the pattern seen in the previous table is confirmed. An individual's escape from low-earning status is positively correlated with that individual having a long commute. The impact overall is highest in the eleven- to twenty-five-mile range, but it is significantly greater than the omitted category (under five miles) at all other distances as well.

Looking at differences between the demographic groups, the relationship between commute distance and escape is strongest in quantitative terms for Asian women and men and weakest for black women and men. Indeed, for black men there is essentially no relationship, and for black women very long commutes are perversely related to escape chances. These relatively weak returns to commuting for blacks have been found

Table 7.4 Distribution of Commuting Distance in California, by Earnings Transition Status

	Still Low Earnings					Full Escapes				
	Under Five Miles	Five to Ten Miles	Eleven to Twenty-Five Miles	Twenty-Six to Fifty Miles	All	Under Five Miles	Five to Ten Miles	Eleven to Twenty-Five Miles	Twenty-Six to Fifty Miles	All
All	0.50	0.23	0.20	0.07	1.00	0.38	0.25	0.27	0.10	1.00
By demographic group										
White female	0.55	0.21	0.18	0.06	1.00	0.42	0.24	0.26	0.09	1.00
Black female	0.40	0.30	0.22	0.08	1.00	0.33	0.29	0.29	0.09	1.00
Asian female	0.54	0.23	0.18	0.05	1.00	0.37	0.27	0.28	0.08	1.00
Hispanic female	0.49	0.24	0.20	0.07	1.00	0.41	0.25	0.25	0.09	1.00
White male	0.45	0.23	0.23	0.09	1.00	0.34	0.24	0.29	0.13	1.00
Black male	0.37	0.25	0.29	0.10	1.00	0.31	0.27	0.28	0.14	1.00
Asian male	0.50	0.24	0.20	0.06	1.00	0.34	0.30	0.27	0.09	1.00
Hispanic male	0.41	0.25	0.25	0.09	1.00	0.34	0.25	0.30	0.11	1.00

Source: Authors' compilation.

Table 7.5 Probability of Escaping Low Earnings Status as a Function of Commuting Distance

	All	White Females	Black Females	Asian Females	Hispanic Females	White Males	Black Males	Asian Males	Hispanic Males
Person effect	1.946	2.208	2.451	2.120	1.694	2.328	2.057	2.014	1.601
	(0.014)*	(0.029)*	(0.094)*	(0.068)*	(0.031)*	(0.048)*	(0.101)*	(0.070)*	(0.031)*
Metropolitan area	0.942	0.895	0.847	0.734	0.992	0.880	0.806	0.779	1.517
	(0.009)*	(0.019)*	(0.040)*	(0.030)*	(0.022)	(0.028)*	(0.050)*	(0.037)*	(0.037)*
Commuting distance[a]									
Five to ten miles	1.213	1.204	1.112	1.361	1.114	1.273	1.221	1.514	1.184
	(0.015)*	(0.027)*	(0.070)	(0.069)*	(0.032)*	(0.048)*	(0.104)*	(0.087)*	(0.370)*
Eleven to twenty-five miles	1.400	1.374	1.210	1.756	1.301	1.421	1.107	1.682	1.385
	(0.017)*	(0.032)*	(0.080)*	(0.092)*	(0.038)*	(0.053)*	(−0.094)	(0.098)*	(0.042)*
More than twenty-five miles	1.280	1.176	0.662	1.491	1.197	1.355	1.067	1.890	1.411
	(0.016)*	(0.027)*	(0.043)*	(0.084)*	(0.036)*	(0.049)*	(0.087)	(0.129)*	(0.044)*
R-squared	0.04	0.05	0.06	0.05	0.02	0.06	0.04	0.05	0.02
Observations	234,109	72,813	8,306	13,464	48,181	24,562	4,712	10,091	36,860

Source: Authors' compilation.

Note: The reported estimates are log-odds ratios. Standard errors are in parentheses.

[a]Under-five-miles category is omitted.

*significant at 1 percent

Table 7.6 Distribution of Average of Firm Effect Within Two Miles, by Earnings Transition Status

Demographic Group	Mean	25th Percentile	Median	75th Percentile
Still low earnings				
White females	−0.108	−0.190	−0.099	−0.020
Black females	−0.043	−0.101	−0.038	0.027
Asian females	−0.061	−0.141	−0.068	0.017
Hispanic females	−0.129	−0.200	−0.087	−0.007
White males	−0.114	−0.200	−0.093	−0.006
Black males	−0.034	−0.111	−0.032	0.039
Asian males	−0.064	−0.141	−0.071	0.014
Hispanic males	−0.209	−0.315	−0.136	−0.038
All	−0.122	−0.198	−0.094	−0.011
Full escapes				
White females	−0.094	−0.177	−0.091	−0.011
Black females	−0.042	−0.110	−0.037	0.035
Asian females	−0.042	−0.134	−0.055	0.038
Hispanic females	−0.076	−0.146	−0.062	0.009
White males	−0.091	−0.179	−0.081	0.003
Black males	−0.042	−0.119	−0.039	0.039
Asian males	−0.040	−0.127	−0.055	0.024
Hispanic males	−0.082	−0.151	−0.068	0.011
All	−0.079	−0.159	−0.072	0.008

Source: Authors' compilation.

elsewhere but do not necessarily run counter to the spatial mismatch hypothesis (Zax 1991).

Tables 7.4 and 7.5 have indicated a positive relationship between escapes from low earnings status and commute distance in the later period. We now turn to the potential impact of the quality of local employers on the escape probability. Table 7.6 shows the quality of the local labor market by demographic group for escapers and non-escapers. This is measured by the average firm wage premia within two miles of a person's home. The table presents both mean results and those at quartiles of the firm fixed effect distribution.

Overall, we see that the quality of local employers was considerably higher for full escapers than for non-escapers, with a value of −0.079 for the former and −.122 for the latter. This strongly suggests that having high-quality local employers is more conducive to escaping low earnings. The biggest differences in local employer quality between escapers and non-escapers were among Asian and Hispanic men and women, while the difference for black women was negligible.

Table 7.7 addresses the same issue by presenting the odds ratios from a logistic regression of transition status on local employer quality, controlling for the individual person effect and metro area location. We see a strong positive relationship between local employer quality and escape probabilities. In other words, this suggests that low earners living near better jobs are more likely to find better jobs. The relationship is as strong for black women as for white women, and as strong for black men as for white men; it is strongest among Hispanics.

Of course, the many factors identified earlier that caused higher earners to live closer to good jobs but have longer commutes may also be relevant for explaining why those who escaped from low earnings also lived closer and commuted farther than those who remained low earners. Our regressions control for person fixed effects but not for other time-varying characteristics of people or employers.

So we conclude this section with the view that there may be a strong spatial basis for part of the differential access to good jobs. Subject to the caveats mentioned earlier, low earners seem more likely to escape into higher earnings if they live in areas with more good jobs nearby or if they can manage longer commutes.

CONCLUSIONS

In this chapter, we have shown that the quality of locally available jobs is significantly and negatively correlated with the fraction of workers who are low-wage workers across geographic areas in several states. This is an important relationship: variations across space in job quality account for a substantial fraction of variations in low earnings status. Taking a dynamic view, we see a strong positive relationship between local employer quality and an individual's chances of escaping low earnings. Longer commutes also improve the odds of escape for low earners.

As we noted earlier, these correlations do not prove that there are causal effects of location on earnings, given the many factors (and potential endogeneities) involved both in where workers choose to live and where employers choose to locate their workplaces. In the appendix, we address this issue, at least partly, by focusing on a particular group of workers (for example, those displaced from their earlier jobs) whose places of residence were probably fixed when they obtained their next job. Our results further suggest that there is a substantial causal connection between geographic locations and employment outcomes for low earners.

A spatial dimension to access to good jobs leads us to consider trans-

Table 7.7 Probability of Escaping Low Earnings Status as a Function of Mean Firm Wage Premia Within Two Miles of Residence

	All	White Females	Black Females	Asian Females	Hispanic Females	White Males	Black Males	Asian Males	Hispanic Males
Person effect	2.057	2.27	2.405	2.200	1.790	2.352	2.078	2.065	1.681
	(0.015)*	(0.030)*	(0.091)*	(0.071)*	(0.034)*	(0.048)*	(0.102)*	(0.071)*	(0.033)*
Metropolitan area	0.769	0.827	0.817	0.725	0.674	0.790	0.759	0.779	0.872
	(0.008)*	(0.018)*	(0.042)*	(0.030)*	(0.017)*	(0.026)*	(0.049)*	(0.036)*	(0.024)*
Labor market quality within:									
Two miles	12.088	3.862	5.892	5.445	45.410	4.456	4.862	2.651	53.321
	(0.533)*	(0.306)*	(1.935)*	(1.144)*	(5.463)*	(0.563)*	(1.934)*	(0.653)*	(6.374)*
Two to five miles	11.027	4.005	4.771	5.018	38.303	4.241	5.593	2.079	52.912
	(0.582)*	(0.373)*	(1.715)*	(1.177)*	(5.448)*	(0.633)*	(2.476)*	(0.569)*	(7.751)*
Six to ten miles	6.265	2.697	6.317	3.243	33.173	2.252	2.904	1.883	57.105
	(0.569)*	(0.426)*	(3.413)*	(1.297)*	(7.852)*	(0.591)*	(1.942)	(0.882)	(13.593)*
R-squared	0.04	0.05	0.06	0.05	0.04	0.06	0.04	0.04	0.05
Observations	234,109	72,813	8,306	13,464	48,181	24,562	4,712	10,091	36,860

Source: Authors' compilation.
Note: The reported estimates are log-odds ratios. Standard errors are in parentheses.
*significant at 1 percent

portation policy as one option to help low earners and job placement efforts more broadly to overcome the information problems also associated with distance. As we note in our final chapter, an emphasis on job placements may entail the use of labor market intermediaries to bridge the locational gaps between low earners and many employers, as well as other gaps (in skills, employer information, and the like) that may be relevant as well.

APPENDIX: MORE ON THE RELATIONSHIP BETWEEN LOCAL LABOR MARKET QUALITY AND EARNINGS OUTCOMES

We have argued in this chapter that distance from good jobs influences earnings outcomes for initial low earners. But it is likely that income and other personal factors also influence an individual's choice of residential location. This problem bedevils the analysis of geographic effects on labor market outcomes.

One potential solution to this problem is to focus on a group of workers for whom residential location is essentially fixed in the short term when they obtain new jobs. To do so, we redo the analysis in this chapter on a sample of workers who appear to be have been displaced from their previous jobs.[8] These workers found themselves looking for a new job in a particular neighborhood, and they chose the neighborhood in relation to the old job.

Restricting our analysis to displaced workers, we present results for workers in Los Angeles County only. In fact, our results are stronger in the statewide analysis (not reported here).[9] We focus our analysis on the impact of local employer quality on an individual's achieved job quality—that is, the fixed effect associated with his or her primary employer. In other words, we regress the wage premium in the job found by the worker on local average employer quality. We look first at all (displaced) workers and then concentrate on (displaced) low earners. For each of these groups, we present results with and without controls for the size of the local labor market. We are interested in the quality of local jobs, and we subdivide the local job quality into three different ranges: jobs within two miles, jobs beyond two miles but within five miles, and jobs beyond five miles but within ten miles.

The results are in table 7A.1. They show considerable support for the idea that location matters for job access. A higher quality of local employers (or better job access) has a significant impact on earnings outcomes. The distance profile suggests that it is in the middle range that distance

Table 7A.1   Effects of Local Firm Wage Premia on Firm Premia of
Newly Hired Workers, Los Angeles County, California

	Displaced Workers		Displaced Low Earners	
	1	2	1	2
Person fixed effect	−0.002 (0.006)	−0.007 (0.006)	0.052 (0.027)	0.054 (0.028)
Mean firm premium at jobs under two miles away	0.479 (0.127)**	0.870 (0.135)**	1.736 (0.245)**	1.571 (0.322)**
Mean firm premium at jobs two to five miles away	0.625 (0.144)**	1.002 (0.151)**	2.386 (0.328)**	2.214 (0.561)**
Mean firm premium at jobs five to ten miles away	0.033 (0.172)	0.510 (0.181)**	1.971 (0.352)**	1.741 (0.565)**
Local demand[a]		0.002 (0.001)*		0.002 (0.003)
Local supply[b]		−0.001 (0.000)**		0.000 (0.000)
Constant	−0.022 (0.005)**	0.071 (0.012)**	−0.278 (0.023)**	−0.310 (0.067)**
Observations	19,640	19,640	1,634	1,634
R-squared	0.02	0.02	0.03	0.03

Source: Authors' compilation.
Note: Standard errors are in parentheses.
[a]"Local demand" is defined for each displaced worker as the total number of new hires within ten miles of residence in 2000.
[b]"Local supply" is defined for each displaced worker as total employment within ten miles of residence in 2000.
*significant at 5 percent; **significant at 1 percent

matters most. Once we control separately for labor market size, the impact of the quality of available jobs increases further.

Thus, while we have not eliminated all potential sources of endogeneity and other biases in our estimated effects of location on earnings outcomes, we have somewhat greater confidence than before that our estimates are capturing causal effects.

Chapter Eight | Conclusions and Policy Implications

To WHAT EXTENT do workers with persistently low earnings advance in the labor market over longer periods of time, and how do they do so? At the outset of this volume, we indicated that economists and other social scientists have had few answers to these questions to date. The role of these workers' access to and employment with high-wage firms, as opposed to their own skills and behavior, has also received only modest attention in previous empirical work on low-wage labor markets. Whether these workers do better by engaging in job retention or in job mobility—staying on their jobs and accumulating experience and on-the-job training versus moving to other (perhaps higher-wage) firms and jobs—has been very unclear to date, and the extent to which the paths to success varied across racial-ethnic or gender groups has been uncertain as well. Furthermore, the benefits of working with intermediaries such as temp agencies or of gaining early work experience even in low-wage jobs that they would ultimately leave were largely unknown, as were the broader characteristics of low-wage employers and their geographic locations.

In this volume, we have attempted to provide some answers to these basic questions. Using the LEHD data—a new dataset compiled by the Census Bureau that provides longitudinal data on nearly universal samples of workers and firms over many years—we have defined samples of prime-age workers who were persistently low earners in five states and have followed them over many subsequent years in the labor market. We have used a three-year base period—1993 to 1995—to define persistent low earners as those who were in the labor market each year but earning less than $12,000 each year. We have tracked their labor market experiences over the subsequent six years (1996 to 2001) to analyze the extent of their transitions out of low earnings and the roles played by person versus employer characteristics and by job retention versus job mobility when they did so.

Here we summarize our main findings from this effort and discuss the implications of this work for policy as well as future research.

SUMMARY OF OUR FINDINGS

There are five main findings from our analysis.

1. *There is considerable mobility out of low earnings status for prime-age adults who have been low earners for at least three years.* This is true even though most transitions are "partial" by our definitions—that is, these workers continue to earn less than $15,000 a year at least some of the time. Transitions out of low earnings and earnings growth more broadly are higher for white males than for other groups. While females consistently have lower transition rates than males in each ethnic group, the gender gaps are greatest among whites (or the race-ethnic gaps are greatest among males). Fixed personal skills and characteristics also matter importantly for earnings growth, with less growth observed among the poorest and least-skilled workers.

2. *Transitions out of low earnings are associated with subsequent employment in high-wage industrial sectors, larger firms, firms with lower turnover, and, especially, high-wage firms.* Even controlling for personal characteristics, the characteristics of the firm have large effects on subsequent earnings. Transition rates are increased a bit in very tight labor markets.

3. *Those who change jobs transition out of low earnings much more frequently than those who stay in jobs.* In fact, job changes account for the vast majority of "complete" transitions out of low earnings and even for most partial transitions. But the highest rates of transition and earnings growth occur for those low earners who change jobs early and then remain with their newer and better employer for a longer time period. Earnings growth is lowest among those who stay with the same (usually) low-wage employer indefinitely. On the other hand, wage growth is impeded over time for those who change jobs perpetually because they have difficulty gaining on-the-job training and accumulating tenure. Wage growth over time is highest at firms that also pay higher wages initially, probably because such firms provide more training and promotion possibilities.

4. *Early work experience at a temp agency is associated with higher subsequent earnings for initial low earners, as is the accumulation of tenure more broadly.* This finding suggests that labor market intermediaries can

play an important role in helping attach low earners to better firms and jobs. It also suggests some modest returns to accumulating stable early work experience and also to working earlier at a higher-wage firm.

5. *There is a great deal of heterogeneity across firms, even within detailed industries and states, in the hiring and advancement opportunities of low earners.* But the firms that provide these opportunities do so persistently and can therefore be identified from past performance. Low earners are also located farther away from good job opportunities than are nonlow earners, and their commuting behavior is more limited. These geographic differences suggest that low earners' access to good jobs may be limited by spatial factors.

Some important caveats should be restated regarding these results. Perhaps our measure of personal skill (the person fixed effect) is not sufficient to fully capture the range of personal characteristics that matter to employers; in that case, the firm effect may proxy for the unmeasured skills that higher-wage employers seek. Empirically, we cannot distinguish here between discrimination against minorities and differences across groups in other unmeasured skills. Differences by gender may still reflect differences in preferences for full-time work. And the firm fixed effect might not persist over time if supplies of skilled workers facing these firms become more ample—though they have persisted to date over many years that capture major fluctuations in local labor market conditions.

Nevertheless, our results—especially when considered in the context of broad literatures that document differential access to firms for minorities and other less-skilled workers—still suggest that firm characteristics and wage premia matter importantly, no matter what other characteristics of workers we control for. Thus, these findings suggest that access to high-wage firms is a critical part of the process by which initial low earners make progress in the labor market. On-the-job training and wage growth are more rather than less likely to occur at these firms.

IMPLICATIONS FOR POLICY: "GOOD JOB" PLACEMENTS AND TRAINING

What does all of this imply for public policies, especially those designed to improve the earnings of persistently low earners over time?

The kinds of policies most frequently advocated for low-earning workers involve some type of remedial education or training. Indeed, many variations of these programs have been developed over the years at the federal, state, and local levels, and a great deal of research and evaluation has gone into these programs.[1] In a labor market where the skill needs of employers have generally been rising over time, and where the returns to skills have risen as well, an emphasis on skill remediation certainly makes sense.[2]

Yet the effects of such remedial programs have often proven to be fairly modest—at least partly because the investments made in training per worker have been fairly limited.[3] Given the recent emphasis on "work-first" in welfare reform, and given the federal budget deficits that will loom over us for many years, it seems unlikely that policy in that realm will shift greatly toward "stand-alone" training (training independent of work experience).

Under these circumstances, we argue for a somewhat different approach, one that integrates the training of lower-income workers with efforts to place them in better jobs. We advocate *a major effort to attach low earners and unskilled workers to better firms and jobs, along with whatever training is needed to get them employed in such firms.*

Since high-wage firms also provide more on-the-job training and promotion possibilities, such efforts appear to generate both higher wage levels initially and higher rates of wage growth over time. The few such efforts made to date—such as the Welfare-to-Work Program administered in Portland, Oregon, in the 1990s—have had impressive returns relative to those of training (or job search assistance) alone.[4]

We also know that the access of some groups of low earners, especially minorities, to high-wage firms and jobs is often quite low. Our analysis suggests that this limited access partly accounts for the higher earnings growth over time of white males relative to other groups. Other analyses, particularly for African Americans, suggests that their access to good jobs has been limited by employer discrimination, poor networks, and "spatial mismatch" as well as low skills and lack of early work experience. Thus, the potential benefits to lower-income minority groups from improving the quality of the jobs available to them are quite substantial. But even for low-income whites, access to better jobs appears to be limited as well and could no doubt be improved.

How can this be accomplished? Labor market intermediaries might be one effective means of doing so. Intermediaries are third-party institutions that work with both employers and employees to improve the quality of "matches" between them by overcoming informational, transportation, and attitudinal barriers. Our results on temp agencies are not definitive, but they suggest that this one type of intermediary has been successful in improving the outcomes associated with low earners. Other studies of temp agencies suggest the same.[5] The improvements in earnings do not come right away, and indeed an initial period of low earnings during which some steady work experience is accumulated may be necessary. Certainly the interests of employers in using temp agencies are not altruistic, and the result may be lower earnings and benefits for workers during that time period.[6] But ultimately there appears to be some return to this investment for the worker as well.

Temp agencies are only one type of intermediary. Others can be nonprofit or for-profit placement organizations, with a variety of characteristics and approaches.[7] The key to their efforts is that they maintain good ties to employers and provide some meaningful screening of the job candidates whom they refer. Indeed, without some such "creaming," it is impossible for these agencies to maintain employer confidence, and they are more likely to be viewed with the same skepticism that employers have of the U.S. Employment Service.[8] To be certain that these efforts are cost-effective requires that more be rigorously evaluated, using random assignment or other such methods that deal with the well-known selection issues involved whenever creaming occurs.[9] But there is certainly cause for some optimism in this regard.

Of course, some intermediaries provide help only with job placements and related services (such as transportation and child care); others stress job retention and advancement as well as placement and view skill upgrading as part of their mission. Since more on-the-job training appears to occur at higher-wage than lower-wage firms, the training intermediaries must provide is whatever is required to get a person hired into any particular firm or job.[10]

Sectoral training strategies—those that focus on training individuals for work in particular sectors of the economy that pay high wages and/or are in high demand in any local area—are also good examples of an approach that integrates training with targeted job placements (Conway and Rademacher 2003). Intermediaries such as the Center for Employment and Training (or CET) in San Jose are well known for targeting major sectors and employers in the local area and molding their training to fit those sectors. Of course, economists generally believe that employers should be more willing to pay for training that is less general and more specific to their own firms (Becker 1975). But even sectoral training can be fairly general in nature and should generate portable skills for a worker who ultimately might move to other firms in that sector or to related sectors of the economy.

For low-income individuals with poor work experience, training and job placements may also need to be *sequential* in nature. In other words, it may be necessary to provide workers with general job-readiness preparation and some initial low-wage job placements before they can move to better firms and jobs. Indeed, the returns to tenure with any earlier employer (see chapter 5) suggest some returns to work experience broadly, as the "work-first" approach would imply. But once these workers gain some initial experience and their job-readiness skills are no longer in doubt, intermediaries might then plan for their placement in better firms and jobs that provide greater hope of upward mobility and career advancement (Martinson and Strawn 2003).

And how can intermediaries (or staff in One-Stop offices) who hope to place low-income workers in better jobs and sectors—either initially or ultimately—determine the right sectors and jobs at the local level? One approach is to gain direct access to the LEHD data at the local level. Since these data, now publicly available at the county level, provide information on hiring and wages for very detailed industries at that level, they can be used to inform local service providers about the local availability of "good jobs," in both the short and long term.[11]

Of course, a wide range of additional policies might also play some role in promoting advancement among low earners, including: remediation strategies for the particular barriers facing these workers, such as mental illness or substance abuse; enhanced use of financial incentives like the EITC; pre- and postemployment support services for workers; and greater assistance with child care or transportation problems. These policies could all be considered complementary to those that we outlined earlier.[12]

IMPLICATIONS FOR POLICY: CREATING MORE "GOOD JOBS"?

Even if such placement efforts are successful and cost-effective, some other objections to them might be raised. For instance, in a labor market with a limited number of high-wage firms and jobs, do efforts to improve the quality of job placements for one group effectively displace another group, generating no net benefit to workers overall? In a labor market where wages for unskilled workers have stagnated or declined for many years and inequality has grown dramatically, are we merely relegating some workers to low-wage jobs when we improve placements for others?[13] And instead of an effort to "ration" these high-wage jobs more equitably, should we instead be trying to create more such good jobs?

On the first issue, it is not at all clear that efforts to improve job placements for some workers create a "zero-sum" game in which some lose as much as others gain. For in improving the efficiency with which workers are matched to jobs, employers' overall employment costs are reduced and therefore more such jobs can be created. For instance, the direct costs to employers of recruiting, screening, and training new workers can be substantial, and in tight labor markets (such as the late 1990s and the conditions we are expecting in coming years as baby boomers retire) job vacancy rates and durations to employers can be high and costly.[14] By improving the quality and especially the speed with which appropriate workers are matched to jobs, these costs can be substantially mitigated for employers. And even if some workers who otherwise might have obtained these high-wage jobs no longer have access to them, net social well-being might certainly be improved by enabling more disadvantaged workers—who otherwise would probably be unemployed—to have access to these jobs.

But is it also possible to generate more such "good jobs"? We can imagine three approaches to this end: government mandates; government encouragement through tax credits and subsidies; or private efforts at the local or industry level to encourage more such behavior among employers.

At the national level, higher minimum wages and reformed labor laws designed to increase collective bargaining are ways of encouraging (or forcing) employers to pay higher wages, though they could generate employment losses if implemented aggressively and on a large scale. Since real minimum wages and the incidence of collective bargaining have both declined substantially over time in the United States, we see little risk of major disemployment effects from these policies anytime soon. At the same time, while we are sympathetic to such efforts, we are also skeptical that either will have widespread new effects on private employers in the foreseeable future.[15]

Other proposals to encourage the growth of higher-wage industries and protect those that already exist—like the "industrial policy" schemes of the 1980s or efforts to block the expansion of international trade—could be legitimately accused of fostering economic inefficiencies and replacing market outcomes with the judgments of bureaucrats. More recent proposals to reward companies for "good behavior"—such as those proposed by former Secretary of Labor Robert Reich in the mid-1990s—might similarly be criticized for discouraging the adjustment mechanisms by which the labor market rewards more-productive firms relative to those that are less productive.[16]

But tax credits and subsidies to firms that provide on-the-job training and advancement opportunities to less-educated workers are, to us, a much more appealing version of this approach. The evidence on their effects from state-level programs in Michigan, California, and elsewhere in the 1980s and 1990s suggests that they can have positive effects on the earnings of less-educated workers as well as on the performance of firms.[17]

At the state and local levels, efforts to lure large and often higher-wage employers often take the form of "economic development" policies that generally entail tax cuts or subsidies to employers. Their effects on employment and economic growth appear to be small—perhaps because states end up in bidding wars over companies that, in this case, really do amount to a zero-sum game.[18]

To encourage more such employers at the local level without engaging in unproductive competition across states and local areas, we once again turn to the concept of labor market intermediaries and their potential effects. Many intermediaries do much more than simply place workers in jobs. In a variety of settings—such as the Casey Foundation's Jobs Initiative, the Wisconsin Training Partnership, Project QUEST in San Antonio, and WIRENet in Cleveland, to name just a few—intermediary organizations work with employers, workers, and training providers (such as community colleges) to change the way labor markets operate more broadly. Enhancing worker skills is almost always an integral part of these efforts, but encouraging employers to develop jobs with higher wages and benefits, training opportunities and career ladders for workers, better recruitment and selection mechanisms, and compensation tied to performance is also included. Some efforts focus more on particular sectors in local labor markets, while others are broader in scope.[19] All are based on the assumption that firms have broad discretion in setting their hiring and compensation policies but that, on their own, they may not be completely "optimizing" (due to imperfect information or coordination difficulties).[20]

It cannot be determined whether these efforts would be successful in generating more high-wage employment opportunities for low earners without, as usual, more rigorous study and evaluation. Results to date appear encouraging, but they must be regarded as preliminary. And whether these efforts can be replicated and brought to significant scale remains unknown as well.[21] Still, these efforts offer our best hope of improving the earnings of workers at a broad level, and they certainly deserve greater experimentation and study.

THE NEED FOR MORE RESEARCH

This discussion makes clear that rigorous evaluation of labor market intermediaries and other efforts to improve the availability of high-wage jobs should be a high priority. But other kinds of empirical analysis would be helpful as well.

For example, it would be useful to replicate the kinds of analysis provided here with better demographic data, especially for specific disadvantaged populations such as high school dropouts, those from poor families, or those with physical or mental health problems. Expansion of the LEHD data and development of other administrative datasets would further enable researchers to carry out these analyses.[22]

Gaining a better sense of what contributes to high wages on the firm side is also essential here. Why do some employers choose high-wage strategies while others choose low-wage ones, even in the same detailed industries and local labor markets? What other personnel policies of firms (such as training) are associated with the decision to be a better employer? Also, why do some employers choose to develop ethnic niches while others do not? And what role in these decisions is played by factors such as changing technologies?

A better understanding of all of these issues would be helpful before we could confidently advocate policies to improve the numbers of such firms and jobs. Some of these analyses might need to be more micro in nature—focusing on specific industries and/or local labor markets—so that we could see how the characteristics of local labor supply influence employer choices and the outcomes associated with them. But the returns to advancing this body of knowledge—in terms of how well labor markets function for low-earning workers and for employers, who will soon be entering an extended period of labor market shortages—could be very high.

Notes

CHAPTER 1

1. The Personal Responsibility and Work Opportunity Act (PRWOA) of 1996 ended the program known as Aid to Families with Dependent Children (AFDC) and established Temporary Assistance for Needy Families (TANF). See Blank and Haskins (2002) for a good review of the new program and empirical evidence on its effects.
2. Most economists attribute these developments to the combination of welfare reform, tight labor markets, and the growth of income supports for the working poor (such as the Earned Income Tax Credit) during the late 1990s.
3. For some good overviews of these earlier efforts and discussions, see the volumes edited by Haveman and Palmer (1982) and by Freeman and Gottschalk (1998). Timothy Bartik (2001) also provides some nice discussion of the various approaches.
4. The classic treatment of earnings growth for youth as they accumulate labor market experience is Mincer (1974). For evidence on the unemployment of youth and how it diminishes as they age, see Freeman and Wise (1982).
5. The most recent evaluations of training programs under the Job Training Partnership Act (JTPA) showed quite high rates of returns for adults but very modest investments in training per person, while those for youth showed no significant (or even negative) effects.
6. The cognitive and noncognitive skills needed for employment and advancement in the labor market—sometimes referred to as "hard" and "soft" skill demands, respectively—are reviewed in Holzer (1996), Moss and Tilly (2001), Bowles, Gintis, and Osborne (2001), and Carneiro and Heckman (2003). The many barriers faced by welfare recipients in their attempts to gain and keep employment are discussed in Danziger et al. (2000) and Holzer and Stoll (2001).
7. There has been some debate in the economics literature on the extent to which returns to job tenure with an employer really reflect tenure per se, as

151

opposed to the quality of the match between employer and employee (see Abraham and Farber 1987; Topel 1991).

8. The Bridges-to-Work and Moving-to-Opportunity demonstrations sponsored by the Department of Housing and Urban Development in the 1990s were two such attempts. The former provided mostly transportation and/or job placement services to inner-city workers, while the latter moved inhabitants of poor inner-city neighborhoods to housing in better neighborhoods. Neither has yet demonstrated clear impacts on employment outcomes for those receiving services (see, for instance, Katz, Kling, and Liebman 2001).

9. For instance, the Jobs Initiative, funded by the Annie E. Casey Foundation, is a major initiative to provide a range of services to both workers and employers in six major urban labor markets. But its impacts have not been carefully evaluated (for descriptive information, see Hebert, St. George, and Epstein 2003). As noted earlier, a broader description of intermediaries and their many functions appears in Giloth (2003).

10. These states are among the first to have submitted their UI wage data to the LEHD project and are the only ones for which nine years of data were available by mid-2002 (by which time our analysis was in full swing).

11. The rationale for this definition is discussed in much more detail in chapter 3.

CHAPTER 2

1. The regressions are of the form: $\ln(\text{earnings})_{ijt} = a + b_i + c_j + d_t + f\text{EXP}_{ijt} + e_{ijt}$, where i, j, and t denote the person, firm, and year, respectively; b and c are the person and firm dummies; d represents year dummies; and EXP represents an experience measure drawn from the UI data. Owing to the left-censoring of the UI data (our sample begins only in 1990), experience is measured as age-imputed education-6 until 1990 for each individual. All variables in the equation appear as deviations from sample means so that the means of estimated person and firm effects for the overall sample equal zero.

2. Specifically, the fixed person and firm effects are identified only from individuals who change firms over time. This assumes that such turnover is exogenous with respect to earnings levels. Also, the estimation of both worker and firm fixed effects implies that the latter can be cleanly separated from the former, though there are circumstances under which this might not be so. For example, individuals might gain portable skills from training at a particular firm that then contribute to their estimated person effect or the firm effect observed for a subsequent employer. Finally, we note that the fixed effects are estimates based on large samples of individuals but also on quite limited numbers of quarters per person or firm, which limits the consistency of the estimates.

CHAPTER 3

1. Since each individual is required to appear in our data in each year of the analysis, we omit those who moved out of state or who dropped out of the labor force for other reasons. We also omit agricultural workers, whose coverage in the UI system varies a great deal across states.

2. Earnings are measured in 1998 dollars. We have used the Consumer Price Index-Urban Workers (CPI-U) to deflate earnings over time. Though this index is known to overstate the rate of inflation over time (see, for example, Schultz 2003), it has no effect on comparisons across groups in earnings or earnings growth in comparable time periods. We also have no data on the pecuniary values of fringe benefits for employees (see chapter 2); however, these data are routinely omitted from calculations of poverty rates and the like. Inclusion of these measures would, if anything, exacerbate measured inequality across groups (Hamermesh 1999).

3. The Earned Income Tax Credit for low-income earners, at its maximum (for custodial parents of two or more children), is worth roughly $4,000 per year. The poverty level for a family of four in 2003 was about $18,000.

4. Empirical evidence from the part of the LEHD subsample that can be matched to the CPS is available in the chapter 4 appendix.

5. Results in this chapter are based on a 10 percent sample of the LEHD data for the relevant states. The total sample size is 1,667,978; for low earners it is 135,236. Standard errors on the measures we report, and on the differences in measures across subgroups, are therefore very small, and all differences that we discuss in the text are statistically significant at the .05 level or better. In subsequent chapters, we base our analysis on the full sample (that is, the universe) of low earners in these states.

6. For our sample of low earners, the seventy-fifth percentile of annual earnings is $8,600; the ninetieth percentile is just over $10,000.

7. Fixed effects for each person are defined using data through 1998. But even for the period 1999 to 2001, low earners were heavily concentrated in the bottom quartile of the fixed-effects distribution.

8. In other words, a high fraction of workers within any given industry might be low earners either because average (mean) wages in the industry are low or because there are large gaps (or variances) in earnings across the groups employed there.

9. Retail trade is a sector with lots of part-time and/or young workers, though other analyses (for example, Krueger and Summers 1987) that use hourly (not quarterly) wages and control for the personal characteristics of workers also show that this is a low-wage sector. However, the high fraction of earnings received in the form of unreported tips might also skew results somewhat in both sets of analyses for this sector.

10. They also account for 44 percent of nonlow earners and over 50 percent of these workers if the financial services are included.

11. In particular, the fraction of workers who were low earners in "food stores" and "miscellaneous retail trade"—which include firms such as supermarkets and department stores, respectively—is only about .13.

12. In particular, they account for 6 percent and 22 percent, respectively, of non-low earners.

13. All else being equal, it is well known that firm size is positively associated with wage levels (see Brown, Medoff, and Hamilton 1990). A variety of factors help to account for this phenomenon, including higher capital intensities, better technologies (creating a higher "ability to pay" by employers), and perhaps greater difficulties directly monitoring worker performance in larger firms.

14. The relationships between firm-specific training, wages, and turnover rates are discussed in Parsons (1986).

15. Firm-level wage premia should also reflect differences across firms in the provision of training and perhaps other elements of personnel policies as well.

16. These results are all consistent with the literature on interindustry wage differences (see, for example, Krueger and Summers 1987).

17. The notion that it might be in the economic interests of employers to pay higher wages is known as the "efficiency wage" hypothesis; for reviews, see Katz (1986) and also Rebitzer (1993). The non-economic reasons are sometimes called "owner utility" or "managerial utility" and might include employers' notions of fairness. Eileen Appelbaum, Annette Bernhardt, and Richard Murnane (2003) note that some employers choose to pay higher wages while others do not for a variety of reasons, including their access to information about alternative human resource policies and local economic and demographic conditions.

18. In the 1970s the literature on the "dual labor market" (for example, Doeringer and Piore 1971) emphasized that some workers have difficulty generating higher earnings because they are concentrated in "secondary" markets with low wages and high turnover as opposed to "primary" markets where wages are high and turnover low. But labor economists had difficulty operationalizing these concepts (for example, determining exactly which firms or sectors are primary and which are secondary) and testing them empirically. Lester Thurow's (1975) notion of "job queues," with women and minorities concentrated at the back of the queues, was similar in spirit.

19. The notion that employer locations in suburban areas disadvantage urban minorities who want jobs there is known as the "spatial mismatch" hypothesis (Ihlanfeldt and Sjoquist 1998). Philip Moss and Chris Tilly (2001) argue that employer desires to avoid black applicants appear to explicitly motivate their locational decisions in some cases, and Joleen Kirschenman and Kathryn

Neckerman (1991) make similar arguments about employer choices of recruitment methods; see also Holzer, Raphael, and Stoll (2000).

20. For general discussions of employer hiring behavior and its effects on labor market opportunities for minorities, see Holzer (1996). The importance of informal hiring has been emphasized by both economists (Rees 1966) and sociologists (Granovetter 1974). Evidence on how affirmative action affects employer recruitment and hiring behavior can be found in Holzer and Neumark (2000).

21. Examples of ethnic group niches would include the concentration of East European Jews in the garment industry in New York City in the early twentieth century and the concentration of the Irish in municipal government in Boston, New York, and elsewhere. For discussions of this issue, see Waldinger (1996). For a less academic review, see Barone (2001).

22. Gary Becker (1971) was the first to argue that employers may discriminate on the basis of race because of the racial composition and preferences of their customers. For evidence on this, see Holzer and Ihlanfeldt (1998).

23. For instance, James Heckman and Brook Payner (1989) document dramatic increases in the presence of blacks in textile mills in South Carolina shortly after the passage of the Civil Rights Act in 1964.

24. See Berman, Bound, and Griliches (1994) for evidence on the effects of technological change on employment and wage inequality in manufacturing.

25. William Julius Wilson (1987) and John Kasarda (1995) have emphasized declining employment in manufacturing as one of the causes of declining employment among black men since the 1970s, even though it was only in the industrial Midwest that black men were heavily concentrated in manufacturing before 1970; see also Bound and Holzer (1993). Kasarda, in particular, presents evidence on the relocation of manufacturing firms from cities in the Northeast and Midwest to suburban areas and the South. For evidence on employer preferences for Hispanics, especially immigrants, over black men, see Kirschenman and Neckerman (1991) and Holzer (1996). George Borjas (1994) reviews evidence on recent trends in immigration and their labor market effects, while Luis Falcon and Edwin Melendez (2001) present evidence on the relatively greater strength of informal networks in job search for Hispanics relative to blacks. The disadvantages experienced by blacks in the informal search process are also highlighted in Holzer (1987b).

26. As unionization has declined in construction, the role of informal hiring and the presence of immigrants (both legal and illegal) have no doubt grown.

27. Holzer (1998) presents strong evidence on the effects of firm size on the hiring of blacks. He argues that smaller firms rely more heavily on informal (and often more discriminatory) hiring methods and that civil rights laws regarding employment are applied less rigorously to smaller firms.

28. In these regressions, the coefficients on all race-gender groups (relative to the

omitted group of white males) are negative and significant. Coefficients for black and Hispanic males indicate average firm wage premia that are .04 to .08 lower than those of white males. Those for white, black, and Hispanic females are .05 to .09 lower than those of white males. In addition, foreign-born workers earned premia about .02 lower than those of native-born workers. The inclusion of the person fixed effects as regressors in these models is questionable, as we discuss in chapter 4; however, their inclusion has very little effect on these estimated coefficients.

CHAPTER 4

1. Of those who were still low earners during the period 1996 to 1998, 57 percent remained low earners in the period 1999 to 2001; this is a lower rate of transition out of low earnings than we observe for the entire sample in the first of these periods. In contrast, of those who partially escaped low-earner status in the 1996 to 1998 period, 38 percent made the full transition to nonlow earnings, and this is a higher rate of transition out of this status than we observe initially.

2. Since we are analyzing increases in earnings that are averaged over three-year periods, the observed rates of increase effectively can be considered increases over six years (from 1994 to 2000) rather than over nine years.

3. Helen Connolly, Peter Gottschalk, and Katherine Newman (2003) use data from the Survey of Income and Program Participation (SIPP) to analyze earnings growth among low earners in the 1980s and 1990s. They follow up on work done by Katherine Newman (1998), who found substantial earnings growth in the late 1990s among a sample of young workers who initially worked for low wages at a fast-food restaurant in New York.

4. For example, median earnings growth for this group was 35 percent between the 1993 to 1995 period and the 1996 to 1998 period.

5. Presenting data from the same quarters across various years—during which time minimum wage increases were implemented in some years but not in others—enables us to infer the effects of the minimum-wage increases without their being contaminated by seasonality.

6. Specifically, transitions from low to partially low and nonlow earnings were higher in North Carolina, the state with the lowest unemployment rate in 2000, than in all other states in our sample except Maryland. But the differences were small: for example, 72 percent of initial low earners transitioned out of this status in North Carolina and Maryland, compared to 68 or 69 percent in the other states. Furthermore, complete transitions to nonlow earnings in North Carolina were lower than elsewhere.

7. For a broad overview of the effects of the minimum wage on the earnings and employment of young workers and those with low incomes, see Card and

Krueger (1997); for an alternative view, see Neumark and Wascher (1998). If minimum-wage increases have contemporaneous or lagged negative effects on employment, then this might lower any observed impacts in figure 4.2 during the fourth quarters of 1996 and 1997 or later. Most estimates of such negative employment effects, however, suggest that they are too small to fully offset any positive effects that might directly result from higher wages.

8. These results imply that the *levels* of earnings depend on the levels of unemployment and that rates of *changes* in earnings depend on changes in (but not levels of) unemployment.

9. Increases in the EITC for low earners were implemented in 1994. The maximum credit per low-income family rose to roughly $4,000 per year. For a discussion and evidence on this issue, see Meyer and Holtz-Eakin (2002).

10. Unfortunately, even though fixed effects measured through 1998 are not explicitly endogenous with respect to earnings for the period 1999 to 2001, those earnings partly reflect earnings growth that occurred during the period 1996 to 1998. Also, as noted in chapter 3, it is impossible to disentangle the effects of skills from discrimination when considering the lower fixed effects observed among women and minorities.

11. While 22 percent of Asian men who completely transitioned out of low earnings did so through retail trade jobs, and 42 percent of those who partially transitioned out did so through this sector, 53 percent of those who remained low earners were employed in retail trade. In most of the other cases noted here, the percentages of those who remained low earners in the service sectors were comparable in magnitude to those who were escaping low earnings.

12. Only 5 percent of black men who remained low earners in the 1999 to 2001 period were employed in manufacturing. The ratio of concentrations in manufacturing for those who escaped low earnings to those who remained in low earnings is higher for black men than for most other groups.

13. Odds ratios represent exponentiated logit coefficients. They are interpreted as the ratio of the odds $(P/1 - P)$ of the event occurring for those with a particular characteristic versus those without it. Ratios above one indicate positive effects of that characteristic on the probability of observing the outcome in question.

14. The earnings measures used in table 4.8 are average annual earnings over the three-year period. The regressions presented in chapter 5 use each person-quarter as a separate observation and thus enable us to avoid having to average earnings across periods.

15. Since race-gender and place of birth are also fixed personal characteristics, it is inappropriate to include them in equations that control for person fixed effects; negative fixed effects for minorities and females may capture unmeasured skills or systematic discrimination against those groups. Also, we have estimated equations for the probability of transitions out of low earnings that

control the earnings of each individual in the base period. The inclusion of the fixed effect in these equations generally eliminated any positive effects of the base period wage and had similar (but stronger) effects on transitions than did the base period wage.

16. Since industry is a fixed firm characteristic and the size and turnover rates are relatively fixed, we do not include them in the same equations as firm fixed effects.

17. We do not consider data on individuals in the CPS beyond the base period, since the wage and earnings outcomes in those years would be likely to reflect the transitions out of low earnings whose determinants we are analyzing here. Instead, our goal in this section is simply to identify low earners in the base period whose personal and family characteristics seem to reflect true disadvantage in the labor market. We also focus on the March CPS, which contains information on annual incomes for the entire family and household over the previous year.

18. The CPS is administered nationally to about 60,000 households each month. However, the sample sizes within the five states we consider here, and especially the sample sizes of prime-age workers who are also low earners in those states, are much smaller.

19. Among prime-age workers with consistent labor market attachment, the variance over time in hourly wages should not be too dramatic as well.

20. Wages and incomes are measured here in 1998 dollars, as they are throughout this analysis.

CHAPTER 5

1. We use the terms "job-changer" and "job-mover" interchangeably here. The latter term is used frequently by economists writing on this topic.

2. On the differences in outcomes between job-to-job turnover and job-to-non-employment, see, for example, Royalty (1998).

3. For evidence of both positive and negative effects on earnings of turnover among young and/or less-skilled workers, see, for example, Ballen and Freeman (1986), Topel and Ward (1992), Gladden and Taber (2000), and Neumark (2002).

4. For the original theory, in which workers who gain general training pay for all such training in the form of lower wages while the costs of specific training are shared between them and the firm, see Becker (1975). For mixed evidence and further discussion of these issues, see Bishop (1994) and Acemoglu and Pischke (1999).

5. In other words, turnover is *endogenous* with respect to opportunities on any particular job relative to the labor market more broadly.

6. For example, there may be mobility involving nonprimary employers during

these time periods that is not captured here. Temporary layoffs and recalls are also not included in our turnover measures. And turnover among both younger and older cohorts of workers are likely to be higher than those measured here for prime-age workers. For evidence on turnover rates more broadly defined, see Anderson and Meyer (1994).

7. The two conditional probabilities are closely related to one another. In particular, the probability of a job change, conditional on a successful transition out of low earnings, equals the probability of success conditional on a job change multiplied by the overall probability of a job change divided by the overall probability of success (according to Bayes's Rule).

8. Note that the samples of low earners differ across the first two periods. The means of complete escape across the two subperiods need not add up, since many complete escapers by the second period had made a partial escape by the first period and are not included in the measured escapes out of low earnings in the second period.

9. As noted earlier, the extent to which such mobility generates periods of non-employment depends on the extent to which individuals have lined up new jobs before they move.

10. In other words, those for whom job turnover is voluntary may already be making optimizing choices for themselves, conditional on their opportunities. Of course, some are leaving their jobs involuntarily, while some voluntary movers may not be fully informed about their opportunities or fully rational. Alternatively, this simply suggests the need to improve the job opportunities over which these individuals choose, as we argue later.

11. A range of evidence shows that blacks are discharged more frequently from their jobs than are whites; their quit rates are also higher, though this differential disappears once wages and other job characteristics are controlled for (see Parsons 1986).

12. The higher turnover of individuals out of high-turnover firms is not completely endogenous (or tautological), since we are looking only at the behavior of low earners, who constitute small percentages of most firms' overall employment and turnover.

13. A great deal of evidence suggests that turnover on the job declines with overall work experience (see Holzer and Lalonde 2000). The accumulation of early work experience may make these workers more stable and productive and may more readily signal job-readiness to employers as well, thus improving future employment prospects.

14. For instance, the person and firm fixed effects are defined on samples of workers and firms through 1998; including years in our current estimation before that point would create some serious endogeneity problems. Also, conditioning our samples on mobility behavior through 1998 would generate

problems for earnings observations prior to 1998, as the mobility would then be endogenous with respect to outcomes for that period.

15. Chow tests we have done reject the pooling of these different mobility samples into one group.

16. We use quadratic terms for overall potential experience as well, and for similar reasons.

17. We have estimated a variety of models for determining the "hazard," or probability of turnover, conditional on person and firm characteristics as well as on turnover. Firm fixed effects generally show negative effects on turnover in these equations. Details are available from the authors.

18. In plotting earnings for each level of tenure, we predict earnings based on all other characteristics of these groups at their mean values along with their relevant coefficients from the earnings regressions. Essentially, these means and coefficients determine the intercepts of the graphs presented, while the graphs themselves reflect the coefficients on the linear and quadratic tenure terms.

19. In other words, when the log of earnings has a constant relationship with quarters of tenure, this indicates a constant growth rate in percentage terms, but the absolute level of growth is higher for higher-wage firms.

20. These decompositions can be performed either using the coefficients of the base group (in this case, stay-stayers) to weight differences in variable means and the means of the other groups to weight differences in coefficients, or vice versa. We have performed the decompositions both ways, and the results are qualitatively similar. We present results here from decompositions using the former combination of means and coefficients.

21. We combine linear and quadratic terms on tenure and on tenure interacted with the firm effect by adding them together.

22. We can interpret the non-interacted effects of tenure as representing those for firms with zero fixed effects, which would reflect firms with average (neither positive nor negative) firm wage premia. We can also interpret the effects of the non-interacted firm effect as representing the effect on wages at zero tenure, or right at the outset of an individual's time with a firm.

23. For example, differences in experience and its returns contribute large negative amounts to the differences in wages between groups of job-movers and the perpetual job-stayers. These large negative amounts are largely offset by positive effects of person fixed effects and large constant terms. The latter can be interpreted as reflecting unobserved differences in either the workers or the firms that are not permanent and therefore not captured by either the person or firm fixed effects.

24. To estimate the effects of earlier tenure on current earnings, we use linear measures of earlier tenure rather than quadratic ones. This makes it easier to interpret the effects of those tenure measures. Also, it is less clear theo-

retically that previous tenure would have a quadratic effect on current earnings.

25. For those who stayed on their initial primary job in the first subsequent period, both the firm fixed effects and the variable measuring work at a temp agency have the same value as in the base period, since the job is the same. Only the tenure measure should change over time, and so we use the one reflecting more recent accumulations.

26. We also estimated equations in which we excluded and then included current tenure in the 1999 to 2001 period, to see whether early work experiences and tenure affect current earnings through their effects on current tenure. But results with and without the measures of current tenure were virtually identical.

27. The effects of working for a temp agency on *contemporaneous* wages are usually negative and sometimes significantly so in estimates that we do not report here, consistent with the general view that temp agencies pay relatively low wages.

28. See Autor and Houseman (2002a) for the effects of temp agencies on the earnings of less-skilled workers using a quasi-experimental research design on data from various One-Stop offices in Michigan. They also find relatively positive effects of working for temp agencies on earnings, even while individuals are working for these agencies. We should also note that, even if temp agencies engage in "creaming" on behalf of their employer-clients, they still may have positive impacts on the earnings of workers who might otherwise not have access to good employment options.

CHAPTER 6

1. In this chapter, we focus on firms that *hire* low earners in a particular time period rather than on those that employ them at a point in time. In other words, we focus on *flows* of low earners in firms rather than stocks. We do so for two reasons. First, a sample of workers hired during a particular time period constitutes a random sample of those workers that neither over- nor underrepresents those with different durations of employment (Kiefer 1988). Second, we are especially interested in low earners who change jobs—the job-movers of the previous chapter. These individuals have substantially higher rates of ultimate labor market success than do those who do not change jobs. For these initial low earners, we want to know more about their job mobility experiences and especially about the kinds of firms that offer them opportunities for subsequent labor market success.

2. The concentrations of low earners hired across and within industries and firms in table 6.1 and figure 6.1 are quite similar to those calculated for all newly hired low earners during the base period 1993 to 1995.

3. In this section, we focus on rates of transition, or "escape," out of low earn-

ings among initial low earners hired in the period 1996 to 1998 and on the employers that hired them *in that period*. In chapter 4, we analyzed the relationship between escapes out of low earnings as of 1999 to 2001 and employers in that period. In this chapter, we focus more on the employers in the intervening period 1996 to 1998 and on escapes in either that period or subsequently, since we are interested in the roles played by employers in helping to generate success either concurrently or later. Most results across the two chapters are quite consistent with one another.

4. Similar concentrations of escapes among firms that hire low earners can also be found if we include partial transitions, as we do later in this section.

5. At this point, we change our definition of "escape" to include those who were partially transitioned out of low earnings as well as those who did so fully.

6. To save space we do not report the same graph for "all industries," but it is very similar to those presented here.

7. In this particular case, "escapes" refer only to those that occurred in the same period as the hiring of low earners. This is necessary in order to analyze escape rates over time for the same firms.

8. As usual, to make this calculation sensible we include only firms that had at least five low-wage hires in the 1996 to 1998 period.

9. It is worth noting that, since these are averages of the firm proportions—and are unweighted—they reflect the rate for the average firm rather than the average worker. Thus, there need not be substantial correspondence between these proportions and those in earlier chapters.

10. In the former set of industries, 55 to 60 percent of escapes occurred with these firms in the 1996 to 1998 period; in the latter set of industries, only 35 to 45 percent of escapes occurred at these firms.

CHAPTER 7

1. The Los Angeles area is defined as Los Angeles County, the Chicago area as Cook County, and the Twin City area as Hennepin and Ramsey counties.

2. The quality of the geocoding is quite good. Approximately 97 percent of all workers and establishments have geocodes that uniquely define the relevant census tract or better. (Within this group, all but a few percent are geocoded to the rooftop.) This allows us to measure workers' and firms' absolute and relative locations with a great deal of accuracy.

3. Multiple imputation techniques are used to link workers to establishments based on a model that takes into account the relative location of workers and establishments, the employment distribution across establishments, and dynamic employment restrictions.

4. Although we carry out the main analysis in this chapter over three different

states, we illustrate the spatial pattern in relation to one state, California. The patterns are similar in the other states.

5. We limit the sample to workers who commute less than fifty miles. According to the data, a small fraction of workers commute even longer distances and sometimes unreasonably long distances. This can happen as a consequence of measurement errors in data associated with, for example, recent changes in residency.

6. See Holzer, Ihlanfeldt, and Sjoquist (1994) for evidence of longer commute times but shorter commute distances among blacks than whites in the 1979 cohort of the National Longitudinal Survey of Youth (NLSY79). The results presented here may be unique to California, or they may be more representative of adults than youth (see also Zax 1991).

7. Some of the logit regression odds ratios, especially those associated with person effects, look very large. But this coefficient is measured in percentage terms, and so small variations in that variable mitigate the apparently large effects on odds of escape.

8. A worker is defined as displaced if he or she was separated from a firm in 1999 while his or her maximum employment at the firm in the two quarters following separation was at least 30 percent lower than in the two quarters preceding the separation.

9. This is based at least partly on differences between urban and rural areas, which are not particularly relevant to the access issue.

CHAPTER 8

1. For a broad description and review of the programs themselves and the evaluation literature, see Lalonde (1995), Friedlander, Greenberg, and Robins (1997), and Heckman, Lalonde, and Smith (1999).

2. Of course, efforts to improve skills would also include efforts that begin much earlier in the life cycle, such as preschool programs, school reform, "school-to-work" programs, tutoring and mentoring programs (such as Big Brothers and Big Sisters), and dropout prevention efforts (like Quantum Opportunities), but our emphasis is on adults.

3. The evaluations of the adult programs in the Job Training Partnership Act showed quite impressive rates of return per dollar spent, but expenditures were too low to generate substantial earnings improvements (see Heckman, Lalonde, and Smith 1999). Although fewer programs seem to work for youth, the Job Corps has been evaluated as successful in the short term, as has the Youth Service Corps (Jastrzab et al. 1997).

4. Portland was one of eleven sites in the National Evaluation of Welfare to Work Strategies (NEWWS), and it showed the most positive results of all sites

in terms of employment and earnings outcomes among welfare recipients. Unlike other sites that emphasized either "work-first" or training approaches, Portland used a combination of the two and encouraged recipients to look for higher-paying jobs instead of taking the first offer they got (see Michalopoulos and Schwartz 2002).

5. See Autor and Houseman (2002a), who are evaluating the use of temp agencies in Michigan using an evaluation strategy that involves random assignment of individuals to temps versus other treatments in certain One-Stop offices.

6. For some discussion of the controversy over temp agencies, and especially over employers' long-term use of temps earning low wages and few benefits, see Autor and Houseman (2002b); see also Lane et al. (2003).

7. Examples of for-profit placement agencies that focus on low-wage workers include America Works. Nonprofits include STRIVE and, with a particular focus on ex-offenders, the Center for Employment Opportunities (New York) and the Safer Foundation (Chicago). Even One-Stop offices can be considered a type of intermediary, though a type that offers little contact with employers besides information on job vacancies.

8. The negative employer perceptions of the U.S. Employment Service have been emphasized in Rees (1966) and Bishop (1993). Despite these broadly negative views, there is some evidence that the Employment Service has been a cost-effective method of placing a limited number of less-skilled workers (see Eberts and Holzer 2004).

9. The fact that placement agencies "cream" does not necessarily mean that they do not have positive impacts on employment, especially if those whom they cream would have greater difficulty achieving access to the same employers on their own.

10. For evidence that temp agencies provide some general skills training to workers whom they are trying to place into jobs, see Autor (2001).

11. The LEHD website is http://lehd.dsd.census.gov.

12. The Employee Retention and Advancement (ERA) evaluation currently being conducted by MDRC is a multi-site attempt to test the impacts of these policies. At least some of its sites involve the kinds of placement and training strategies we advocate here (for a description, see Bloom et al. 2002).

13. The evidence on the growth of labor market inequality in the 1980s and early 1990s is reviewed in Danziger and Gottschalk (1995).

14. For evidence on the costs associated with recruiting and vacancies, as well as the effects of higher wages in reducing these costs, see Holzer (1990).

15. Minimum wage increases are unlikely to affect wages in the vast majority of establishments, as the data in chapter 4 suggested, and the long-term downward trends in private-sector collective bargaining coverage seem unlikely to be reversed anytime soon.

16. For instance, Secretary Reich proposed subsidies (or tax credits) for firms that avoid large layoffs and plant closures in 1995–96.

17. For evidence on the effects of state-level programs in Michigan and California, see Holzer et al. (1993) and Moore et al. (2003), respectively. For more general evidence on the positive effects of firm-level education on low-wage workers, see Ahlstrand, Bassi, and McMurrer (2003).

18. For more discussion on local economic development policies, see Bartik (2001). Other kinds of development policies, such as tax credits for training, induce much less of this wasteful interstate competition (for an example, see Holzer et al. 1993).

19. For more discussion on intermediaries and the range of activities that they undertake, see Giloth (2003). For examples of approaches that focus on specific sectors and examine why they may work particularly well, see Aspen Institute (2002). For an excellent review of new hiring and compensation policies across different sectors of the economy, see Appelbaum, Bernhardt, and Murnane (2003).

20. See Abowd et al. (2003) for evidence that firms "learn" over time in ways that enhance their productivity and odds of survival, instead of correctly "optimizing" at all times.

21. In terms of scale, the Jobs Initiative has been a $30 million effort involving thousands of workers and their employers in six major cities, but evaluation to date has primarily involved before-after comparisons of earnings without any use of comparison or control groups (see Hebert, St. George, and Epstein 2003).

22. When more states have been integrated into the LEHD data, the sample sizes of the data matched to the CPS and other sources will be great enough to allow for more extensive analysis of demographic groups. Merging of the LEHD data with other administrative files at the state level, such as those for welfare recipients, will also be very helpful. The use of administrative data to study groups such as ex-offenders in the labor market has been developed as well (see Kling and Tyler 2002; Pettit and Lyons 2002).

References

Abowd, John. 2002. "Unlocking the Information in Integrated Social Data." New Zealand Economic Papers 0077-9954, 36, 1, 9–31.

Abowd, John, John Haltiwanger, Ron Jarmin, Julia Lane, Paul Lengermann, Kristin McCue, Kevin McKinney, and Kristin Sandusky. 2003. "The Relation Among Human Capital, Productivity, and Market Value: Building Up from Micro Evidence." In Measuring Capital in the New Economy, edited by Carol Corrado, John Haltiwanger, and Dan Sichel. Chicago: University of Chicago Press.

Abowd, John, and Francis Kramarz. 1999. "The Analysis of Labor Markets Using Matched Employer-Employee Data." In The Handbook of Labor Economics, vol. 3B, edited by Orley Ashenfelter and David Card. Amsterdam: North Holland.

Abowd, John, Paul Lengermann, and Kevin McKinney. 2003. "The Measurement of Human Capital in the U.S. Economy." LEHD Technical Paper TP-2002-03. Washington: U.S. Census Bureau.

Abowd, John, and Lars Vilhuber. 2004. "The Sensitivity of Economic Statistics to Coding Errors in Personal Identifiers." Journal of Business and Economic Statistics, forthcoming.

Abraham, Katherine, and Henry Farber. 1987. "Job Duration, Seniority, and Earnings." American Economic Review 77(2): 278–97.

Acemoglu, Daron, and Jorn-Steffen Pischke. 1999. "Beyond Becker: Training in Imperfect Labor Markets." Economic Journal Features 109(453): F112–42.

Ahlstrand, Amanda, Laurie Bassi, and Daniel McMurrer. 2003. Workplace Education for Low-Wage Workers. Kalamazoo, Mich.: W. E. Upjohn Institute for Employment Research.

Allard, Scott, and Sheldon Danziger. 2003. "Proximity and Opportunity: How Residence and Race Affect Welfare Recipients." Housing Policy Debate 13(4): 675–700.

Anderson, Patricia, and Bruce Meyer. 1994. "The Extent and Consequences of Job Turnover." Brookings Papers on Economic Activity Microeconomics: 177–248.

Andersson, Fredrik, Harry Holzer, and Julia Lane. 2003. "Worker Advancement in the Low-Wage Labor Market: The Importance of 'Good Jobs.'" Washington, D.C.: Brookings Institution, Center on Urban and Metropolitan Policy.

Appelbaum, Eileen, Annette Bernhardt, and Richard Murnane. 2003. *Low-Wage America.* New York: Russell Sage Foundation.

Aspen Institute. 2002. *Grow Faster Together or Grow Slowly Apart.* Washington, D.C.: Aspen Institute, Domestic Strategy Group.

Autor, David. 2001. "Why Do Temporary Help Firms Provide Free General Skills Training?" *Quarterly Journal of Economics* 116(4): 1409–48.

Autor, David, and Susan Houseman. 2002a. "Do Temporary Help Jobs Improve Labor Market Outcomes? A Pilot Analysis with Welfare Clients." Unpublished paper. Massachusetts Institute of Technology.

———. 2002b. "The Role of Temporary Employment Agencies in Welfare to Work: Part of the Problem or Part of the Solution?" *Focus* 22(1): 63–70.

Autor, David, Lawrence Katz, and Alan Krueger. 1998. "Computing Inequality: Have Computers Changed the Labor Market?" *Quarterly Journal of Economics* 113(4): 1169–1214.

Ballen, John, and Richard Freeman. 1986. "Transitions Between Employment and Non-employment." In *The Black Youth Employment Crisis,* edited by Richard Freeman and Harry J. Holzer. Chicago: University of Chicago Press.

Barone, Michael. 2001. *The New Americans.* Washington, D.C.: Regnery.

Bartel, Ann, and George Borjas. 1981. "Wage Growth and Job Turnover: An Empirical Analysis." In *Studies in Labor Markets,* edited by Sherwin Rosen. Chicago: University of Chicago Press.

Bartik, Timothy. 2001. *Jobs for the Poor.* New York: Russell Sage Foundation.

Becker, Gary. 1971. *The Economics of Discrimination.* Chicago: University of Chicago Press.

———. 1975. *Human Capital.* Chicago: University of Chicago Press.

Berman, Eli, John Bound, and Zvi Griliches. 1994. "Changes in the Demand for Skilled Labor Within U.S. Manufacturing." *Quarterly Journal of Economics* 109(2): 367–98.

Bishop, John. 1993. "Improving Job Matches in the U.S. Labor Market." *Brookings Papers on Economic Activity* Microeconomics(1): 335–90.

———. 1994. "The Incidence and Payoff to Employer Training." Working paper. Ithaca, N.Y.: Cornell University, Center for Advanced Human Resource Studies.

Blank, Rebecca. 1998. "Contingent Work in a Changing Labor Market." In *Generating Jobs: How to Increase Demand for Less-Skilled Workers,* edited by Richard Freeman and Peter Gottschalk. New York: Russell Sage Foundation.

———. 2003. "Evaluating Welfare Reform in the United States." *Journal of Economic Literature* 40(4): 1105–66.

Blank, Rebecca, and Ronald Haskins. 2002. *The New World of Welfare.* Washington, D.C.: Brookings Institution.

Blinder, Alan. 1973. "Wage Discrimination: Reduced Form and Structural Estimates." *Journal of Human Resources* 8(2): 436–55.

Bloom, Dan, Jacquelyn Anderson, Melissa Wavelet, Karen Gardiner, and Michael

Fishman. 2002. *New Strategies to Promote Stable Employment and Career Progression.* New York: MDRC.

Borjas, George. 1994. "The Economics of Immigration." *Journal of Economic Literature* 32(4): 1667–1717.

Bound, John, and Richard Freeman. 1992. "What Went Wrong? The Erosion of Black Relative Wage Gains." *Quarterly Journal of Economics* 107(1): 201–32.

Bound, John, and Harry Holzer. 1993. "Industrial Shifts, Skill Levels, and the Labor Market for White and Black Males." *Review of Economics and Statistics* 75(3): 387–94.

Bowles, Samuel, Herbert Gintis, and Melissa Osborne. 2001. "The Determinants of Earnings: A Behavioral Approach." *Journal of Economic Literature* 39(4): 1137–76.

Brown, Charles, James Medoff, and James Hamilton. 1990. *Employers Large and Small.* Cambridge, Mass.: Harvard University Press.

Burtless, Gary. 1995. "The Employment Prospects of Welfare Recipients." In *The Work Alternative: Welfare Reform and the Realities of the Job Market,* edited by Demetra Smith Nightingale and Robert H. Haveman. Washington, D.C.: Urban Institute.

Cancian, Maria, and Daniel Meyer. 2000. "Work After Welfare: Women's Work Effort, Occupational and Economic Well-being." *Social Work Research* 24(2): 69–86.

Card, David, and Alan Krueger. 1997. *The Minimum Wage: Myth and Measurement.* Princeton, N.J.: Princeton University Press.

Carneiro, Pedro, and James Heckman. 2003. "Human Capital Policy." Working paper 9495. Cambridge, Mass.: National Bureau of Economic Research.

Connolly, Helen, Peter Gottschalk, and Katherine Newman. 2003. "Wage Trajectories of Workers in Poor Households: The National Experience." Unpublished paper. Boston College and Harvard University.

Conway, Maureen, and Ida Rademacher. 2003. "Industry-Specific Workforce Development: Key Research Findings and Implications for the Workforce Investment Act." Washington, D.C.: Aspen Institute, Workforce Strategies Initiative.

Currie, Janet, and Aaron Yelowitz. 2000. "Health Insurance and Less-Skilled Workers." In *Finding Jobs: Work and Welfare Reform,* edited by David Card and Rebecca Blank. New York: Russell Sage Foundation.

Danziger, Sandra, Mary Corcoran, Sheldon Danziger, Colleen Heflin, Ariel Kalil, Judith Levine, Daniel Rosen, Kristin Seefeldt, Kristine Seifert, and Richard Tolman. 2000. "Barriers to the Employment of Welfare Recipients." In *Prosperity for All? The Economic Boom and African Americans,* edited by Robert Cherry and William M. Rodgers III. New York: Russell Sage Foundation.

Danziger, Sheldon, and Peter Gottschalk. 1995. *America Unequal.* New York: Russell Sage Foundation.

Doeringer, Peter, and Michael Piore. 1971. *Internal Labor Markets and Manpower Analysis.* Lexington, Mass.: Heath.

Eberts, Randall, and Harry Holzer. 2004. "Overview of Labor Exchange Policies and Services." In *Labor Exchange Policy in the United States: History, Effectiveness, and Prospects,* edited by David Balducci, Randall Eberts, and Christopher O'Leary. Kalamazoo, Mich.: W. E. Upjohn Institute for Employment Research.

Ellwood, David. 1982. "Teenage Unemployment: Permanent Scars or Temporary Blemishes?" In *The Youth Labor Market Problem: Its Nature, Causes, and Consequences,* edited by Richard Freeman and David Wise. Chicago: University of Chicago Press.

Falcon, Luis, and Edwin Melendez. 2001. "Racial and Ethnic Differences in Job Searching in Urban Centers." In *Urban Inequality: Evidence from Four Cities,* edited by Alice O'Connor, Chris Tilly, and Lawrence D. Bobo. New York: Russell Sage Foundation.

Farber, Henry. 1999. "Mobility and Stability: The Dynamics of Job Change in Labor Markets." In *The Handbook of Labor Economics,* vol. 3B, edited by Orley Ashenfelter and David Card. Amsterdam: North Holland.

Freeman, Richard, and Peter Gottschalk, eds. 1998. *Generating Jobs: How to Increase Demand for Less-Skilled Workers.* New York: Russell Sage Foundation.

Freeman, Richard, and James Medoff. 1984. *What Do Unions Do?* New York: Basic.

Freeman, Richard, and David Wise, eds. 1982. *The Youth Labor Market Problem: Its Nature, Causes, and Consequences.* Chicago: University of Chicago Press.

Friedlander, Daniel, David Greenberg, and Philip Robins. 1997. "Evaluating Government Training Programs for the Economically Disadvantaged." *Journal of Economic Literature* 35(4): 1809–55.

Giloth, Robert, ed. 2003. *Workforce Intermediaries for the Twenty-first Century.* New York: Columbia University, American Assembly.

Gladden, Tricia, and Christopher Taber. 2000. "Wage Progression Among Less-Skilled Workers." In *Finding Jobs: Work and Welfare Reform,* edited by David Card and Rebecca Blank. New York: Russell Sage Foundation.

Granovetter, Mark. 1974. *Finding a Job.* Cambridge, Mass.: Harvard University Press.

Haltiwanger, John, Julia Lane, and James Spletzer. 1999. "Productivity Differences Across Employers: The Role of Employer Size, Age, and Human Capital." *American Economic Review* 89(2): 94–98.

Haltiwanger, John, Julia Lane, James Spletzer, Jules Theuwes, and Kenneth Troske. 1999. *The Creation and Analysis of Employer-Employee Matched Data.* Amsterdam: North Holland.

Hamermesh, Daniel. 1999. "Changing Inequality in Markets for Workplace Amenities." *Quarterly Journal of Economics* 114(4): 1085–1124.

Haveman, Robert, and John L. Palmer, eds. 1982. *Jobs for Disadvantaged Workers.* Washington, D.C.: Brookings Institution.

Hebert, Scott, Ann St. George, and Barbara Epstein. 2003. "Breaking Through: Overcoming Barriers to Family-Sustaining Employment." Baltimore: Annie E. Casey Foundation.

Heckman, James, Robert Lalonde, and Jeffrey Smith. 1999. "The Economics and Econometrics of Active Labor Market Programs." In *The Handbook of Labor Economics,* vol. 3A, edited by Orley Ashenfelter and David Card. Amsterdam: North Holland.

Heckman, James, and Brook Payner. 1989. "Determining the Impact of Federal Antidiscrimination Policy on the Economic Status of Blacks: A Study of South Carolina." *American Economic Review* 79(1): 138–77.

Hershey, Alan, and Donna Pavetti. 1997. "Turning Job Finders into Job Keepers." *The Future of Children* 7(1): 74–86.

Holzer, Harry J. 1987a. "Hiring Procedures in the Firm." In *Human Resources and Firm Performance,* edited by Mortis Kleiner, Richard Block, and Myron Roomkin. Madison, Wisc.: Industrial Relations Research Association.

———. 1987b. "Informal Job Search and Black Youth Unemployment." *American Economic Review* 77(2): 446–52.

———. 1990. "Wages, Employer Costs, and Employee Performance in the Firm." *Industrial and Labor Relations Review* 43(3): S147–64.

———. 1996. *What Employers Want: Job Prospects for Less-Educated Workers.* New York: Russell Sage Foundation.

———. 1998. "Why Do Small Employers Hire Fewer Blacks Than Larger Ones?" *Journal of Human Resources* 33(4): 896–914.

Holzer, Harry J., Richard Block, Marcus Cheatham, and Jack Knott. 1993. "Are Training Subsidies for Firms Effective? The Michigan Experience." *Industrial and Labor Relations Review* 46(4): 625–36.

Holzer, Harry J., and Keith R. Ihlanfeldt. 1998. "Customer Discrimination and Employment Outcomes for Minority Workers." *Quarterly Journal of Economics* 113(3): 835–68.

Holzer, Harry J., Keith Ihlanfeldt, and David Sjoquist. 1994. "Work, Search, and Travel Among White and Black Youth." *Journal of Urban Economics* 35: 325–45.

Holzer, Harry J., and Robert J. Lalonde. 2000. "Job Change and Job Stability Among Less-Skilled Young Workers." In *Finding Jobs: Work and Welfare Reform,* edited by David Card and Rebecca Blank. New York: Russell Sage Foundation.

Holzer, Harry J., Julia Lane, and Lars Vilhuber. 2003. "Escaping Low Earnings: The Role of Employers and Their Characteristics." Discussion paper. Madison, Wisc.: Institute for Research on Poverty.

Holzer, Harry J., and David Neumark. 2000. "Assessing Affirmative Action." *Journal of Economic Literature* 38(3): 483–568.

Holzer, Harry J., and Paul Offner. 2002. "Recent Trends in Employment Among Young Men." Discussion paper. Madison, Wisc.: Institute for Research on Poverty.

Holzer, Harry J., Steven Raphael, and Michael Stoll. 2000. "Are Suburban Firms More Likely to Discriminate Against African Americans?" *Journal of Urban Economics* 48(4): 485–508.

————. 2004. "Will Employers Hire Ex-Offenders?" In *The Impacts of Mass Incarceration on Families and Communities,* edited by Mary Pattillo, David Weiman, and Bruce Western. New York: Russell Sage Foundation.

Holzer, Harry J., and Michael Stoll. 2001. *Employers and Welfare Recipients: The Effects of Welfare Reform in the Workplace.* San Francisco: Public Policy Institute of California.

Holzer, Harry J., Michael Stoll, and Douglas Wissoker. 2001. "Job Performance and Retention Among Welfare Recipients." Discussion paper. Madison, Wisc.: Institute for Research on Poverty.

Ihlanfeldt, Keith, and David Sjoquist. 1998. "The Spatial Mismatch Hypothesis: A Review of Recent Studies and Their Implications for Welfare Reform." *Housing Policy Debate* 9(4): 849–92.

Jacobson, Louis, Robert Lalonde, and Daniel Sullivan. 1993. "Earnings Losses of Displaced Workers." *American Economic Review* 83(4): 685–709.

Jastrzab, Joann, John Blomquist, Julie Masker, and Larry Orr. 1997. *Youth Corps: Promising Strategies for Young People and Their Communities.* Cambridge, Mass.: Abt Associates.

Johnson, Rucker. 2002. "Essays on Urban Spatial Structure, Job Search, and Job Mobility." Ph.D. diss., University of Michigan.

Kasarda, John. 1995. "Industrial Restructuring and the Changing Locations of Jobs." In *State of the Union: America in the 1990s,* edited by Reynolds Farley. New York: Russell Sage Foundation.

Katz, Lawrence. 1986. "Efficiency Wages: A Partial Evaluation." *Macroeconomics Annual* (National Bureau of Economic Research, Cambridge, Mass.), vol. 1.

Katz, Lawrence, Jeffrey Kling, and Jeffrey Liebman. 2001. "Moving to Opportunity in Boston: Early Results of a Randomized Mobility Experiment." *Quarterly Journal of Economics* 116(2): 607–54.

Kiefer, Nicholas. 1988. "Economic Duration Data and Hazard Functions." *Journal of Economic Literature* 26: 646–79.

Kirschenman, Joleen, and Kathryn Neckerman. 1991. "'We'd Love to Hire Them But. . . .'" In *The Urban Underclass,* edited by Christopher Jencks and Paul E. Peterson. Washington, D.C.: Brookings Institution.

Kling, Jeffrey, and John Tyler. 2002. "What Is the Value of a Prison GED?" Unpublished paper. Princeton University, Princeton, N.J.

Krueger, Alan, and Lawrence Summers. 1987. "Reflections on the Inter-Industry Wage Structure. " In *Unemployment and the Structure of Labor Markets,* edited by Kevin Lang and Jonathan S. Leonard. New York: Basil Blackwell.

Lalonde, Robert J. 1995. "The Promise of Public-Sector Training Programs." *Journal of Economic Perspectives* 9(2): 149–68.

Lane, Julia. 2000. "The Role of Job Turnover in the Low-Wage Labor Market." In *The Low-Wage Labor Market: Challenges and Opportunities for Economic Self-*

sufficiency, edited by Kelleen Kaye and Demetra Smith Nightingale. Washington, D.C.: Urban Institute.

Lane, Julia, Kelly Mikelson, Pat Sharkey, and Douglas Wissoker. 2003. "Pathways to Work for Low-Income Workers: The Effect of Work in the Temporary Help Industry." *Journal of Policy Analysis and Management* 22(4): 581–98.

Martinson, Karin, and Julie Strawn. 2003. *Built to Last: Why Skills Matter for Long-Run Success in Welfare Reform.* Washington, D.C.: Center on Law and Social Policy.

Melendez, Edwin. 1996. *Working on Jobs: The Center for Employment Training.* Boston: Gaston Institute.

Meyer, Bruce, and Douglas Holtz-Eakin, eds. 2002. *Making Work Pay.* New York: Russell Sage Foundation.

Meyer, Bruce, and Daniel Rosenbaum. 2001. "Welfare, the Earned Income Tax Credit, and the Labor Supply of Single Mothers." *Quarterly Journal of Economics* 116(3): 1063–1114.

Meyer, Robert, and David Wise. 1982. "High School Preparation and Early Labor Force Experience." In *The Youth Labor Market Problem: Its Nature, Causes, and Consequences,* edited by Richard Freeman and David Wise. Chicago: University of Chicago Press.

Michalopoulos, Charles, and Christine Schwartz. 2002. *What Works Best for Whom: Impacts of Welfare-to-Work Programs by Subgroup.* Washington: U.S. Department of Health and Human Services.

Mieszkowski, Peter, and Edwin Mills. 1993. "The Causes of Metropolitan Suburbanization." *Journal of Economic Perspectives* 7(3): 135-48.

Mincer, Jacob. 1974. *Schooling, Experience, and Earnings.* New York: National Bureau of Economic Research.

Moore, Richard, Daniel Blake, Michael Phillips, and Daniel McConaughy. 2003. *Training That Works: Lessons from California's Employment Training Panel Program.* Kalamazoo, Mich.: W. E. Upjohn Institute for Employment Research.

Moss, Philip, and Chris Tilly. 2001. *Stories Employers Tell.* New York: Russell Sage Foundation.

Neumark, David. 2002. "Youth Labor Markets in the United States: Shopping Around Versus Staying Put." *Review of Economics and Statistics* 84(3): 462–82.

Neumark, David, and William Wascher. 1998. "Minimum Wages and Employment: A Case Study of the Fast-Food Industry in New Jersey and Pennsylvania: Comment." *American Economic Review* 90(5): 1362–96.

Newman, Katherine. 1998. *No Shame in My Game.* New York: Russell Sage Foundation.

Oaxaca, Ronald. 1973. "Male-Female Wage Differentials in Urban Labor Markets." *International Economic Review* 14(3): 693–709.

Parsons, Donald. 1986. "The Employment Relationship: Job Attachment, Work Effort, and the Nature of Contracts." In *The Handbook of Labor Economics,* vol. 2, edited by Orley Ashenfelter and Richard Layard. Amsterdam: North Holland.

Pettit, Becky, and Christopher Lyons. 2002. "The Consequences of Incarceration on Employment and Earnings: Evidence from Washington State." Unpublished paper. University of Washington, Seattle.

Raphael, Steven. 1998. "The Spatial Mismatch Hypothesis and Black Youth Joblessness: Evidence from the San Francisco Bay Area." *Journal of Urban Economics* 43(1): 79–111.

Rebitzer, James. 1993. "Radical Political Economy and the Economics of Labor Markets." *Journal of Economic Literature* 31(3): 1394–1471.

Rees, Albert. 1966. "Information Networks in Labor Markets." *American Economic Review* 56(2): 559–66.

Royalty, Ann. 1998. "Job-to-Job and Job-to-Non-Employment Turnover by Gender and Education Level." *Journal of Labor Economics* 16(2): 392–443.

Schultz, Charles. 2003. "The Consumer Price Index: Conceptual Issues and Practical Suggestions." *Journal of Economic Perspectives* 17(1): 3–22.

Stoll, Michael, Harry Holzer, and Keith Ihlanfeldt. 2000. "Within Cities and Suburbs: Racial Residential Concentration and the Spatial Distribution of Employment Opportunities Across Submetropolitan Areas." *Journal of Policy Analysis and Management* 19: 207–32.

Strawn, Julie, Mark Greenberg, and Steven Savner. 2001. "Improving Employment Outcomes Under TANF." In *The New World of Welfare,* edited by Rebecca Blank and Ron Haskins. Washington, D.C.: Brookings Institution.

Thurow, Lester. 1975. *Generating Inequality.* Cambridge, Mass.: Harvard University Press.

Topel, Robert. 1991. "Specific Capital, Mobility, and Wages: Wage Rise with Job Seniority." *Journal of Political Economy* 99(1): 145–76.

Topel, Robert, and Michael Ward. 1992. "Job Mobility and the Careers of Young Men." *Quarterly Journal of Economics* 107(4): 439–79.

Travis, Jeremy, Amy L. Solomon, and Michelle Waul. 2001. "From Prison to Home: The Dimensions and Consequences of Prison Reentry." Report. Washington, D.C.: Urban Institute (June 1).

U.S. Department of Labor. Bureau of Labor Statistics. 1997. *Bureau of Labor Statistics Handbook of Methods.* Washington: U.S. Government Printing Office.

Waldinger, Roger. 1996. *Still the Promised City?* Cambridge, Mass.: Harvard University Press.

Wilson, William Julius. 1987. *The Truly Disadvantaged.* Chicago: University of Chicago Press.

———. 1996. *When Work Disappears.* New York: Alfred A. Knopf.

Yinger, John. 1995. *Closed Doors, Opportunities Lost.* New York: Russell Sage Foundation.

Zax, Jeffrey. 1991. "Compensation for Commutes in Labor and Housing Markets." *Journal of Urban Economics* 30(2): 192–207.

Index

Boldface numbers refer to figures and tables.